Wild Game

WILD

My Mother, Her Lover, and Me

GAME

ADRIENNE BRODEUR

Houghton Mifflin Harcourt
Boston New York
2019

hmhco.com

Library of Congress Cataloging-in-Publication Data
Names: Brodeur, Adrienne, author.
Title: Wild game : my mother, her lover, and me / Adrienne Brodeur.
Description: Boston : Houghton Mifflin Harcourt, [2019].
Identifiers: LCCN 2019004915 (print) | LCCN 2019013400 (ebook) |
ISBN 9781328519047 (ebook) | ISBN 9781328519030 (hardcover) |
ISBN 9780358272670 (PA, Canada edition)
Subjects: LCSH: Brodeur, Adrienne. | Brodeur, Adrienne — Family. |
Hornblower, Malabar. | Mothers and daughters — United States — Biography. |
Authors, American — Biography.
Classification: LCC PS3602.R6346 (ebook) |
LCC PS3602.R6346 Z46 2019 (print) | DDC 813/.6 [B] — dc23
LC record available at https://lccn.loc.gov/2019004915

Book design by Emily Snyder

Printed in the United States of America
DOC 10 9 8 7 6 5 4 3 2 1

"Gott spricht zu jedem . . . / God speaks to each of us . . ." from *Rilke's Book of
Hours: Love Poems to God* by Rainer Maria Rilke, translated by Anita Barrows
and Joanna Macy, translation copyright © 1996 by Anita Barrows and Joanna
Macy. Used by permission of Riverhead, an imprint of Penguin Publishing
Group, a division of Penguin Random House LLC. All rights reserved.

"The Uses of Sorrow," from *Thirst* by Mary Oliver, published by
Beacon Press, Boston. Copyright © 2004 by Mary Oliver, used herewith
by permission of the Charlotte Sheedy Literary Agency, Inc.

For Tim, Madeleine, and Liam
and in memory of Alan

AUTHOR'S NOTE

*Life is not what one lived, but what one remembers and
how one remembers it in order to recount it.*
— GABRIEL GARCÍA MÁRQUEZ

In writing this book, I've endeavored to be as factual as possible,
turning to journals, letters, scrapbooks, photo albums, report cards,
recipes, articles, and other records of my personal and familial history. But in instances where I could not substantiate a physical or
emotional detail, I turned to memory, knowing full well that it is
revisionist and that each time we remember something, we alter it
slightly, massaging our perspective and layering it with new understanding in order to make meaning in the present.

Wild Game does not pretend to tell the whole story — years have
been compressed into sentences, friends and lovers edited out, details scrubbed. Time has scattered particulars. What follows in these
pages are recollections, interpretations, and renderings of moments
that shaped my life, all subject to perspective, persuasion, and longing. I am aware that others may recall things differently and have
their own versions of events. I've tried to be careful in telling a story
that includes other people who may remember or have experienced
things differently.

I have changed the names of everyone in the book except for my
parents, Malabar and Paul, and myself.

THE USES OF SORROW
by Mary Oliver

(In my sleep I dreamed this poem)

Someone I loved once gave me
a box full of darkness.

It took me years to understand
that this, too, was a gift.

PROLOGUE

A BURIED TRUTH, that's all a lie really is.

Cape Cod is a place where buried things surface and disappear again: wooden lobster pots, the vertebrae of humpback whales, chunks of frosted sea glass. One day there's nothing; the next, the cyclical forces of nature—erosion, wind, and tide—unearth something that has been there all along. A day later, it's gone.

A few years ago, my brother discovered the bow of a shipwreck looming from a sandbar. He managed to excavate an ample wedge of hull before the tide came in and thwarted his efforts. The following day, he returned to the same spot at the same tide, but all traces of the ship had vanished. Had he not saved that waterlogged slab of wood, knotted and beautifully gnarled, and left it to dry on his lawn, he might have imagined he'd dreamed the whole thing.

Blink, and you'll miss your treasure.

Blink again, and you'll realize that the truth you thought was safely hidden has materialized, some ungainly part of it revealed under new conditions. We all know the adage that one lie begets the next. Deception takes commitment, vigilance, and a very good memory. To keep the truth buried, you must tend to it.

For years and years, my job was to pile on sand — fistfuls, shovelfuls, bucketfuls, whatever the moment necessitated — in an effort to keep my mother's secret buried.

PART I

Oh, what a tangled web we weave.

— SIR WALTER SCOTT

ONE

BEN SOUTHER PUSHED through the front door of our Cape Cod beach house on a hot July evening in 1980, greeting our family with his customary, enthusiastic "How do!" In his early sixties at the time, Ben had a full head of thick, white hair and callused hands that broadcast his love of outdoor work. I watched from the hallway as he back-patted my stepfather, Charles Greenwood, with one hand and, with the other, raised high a brown paper grocery bag, its corners softening into damp, dark patches.

"Let's see what you can do with these, Malabar," Ben said to my mother, who stood in the entryway beside her husband. He presented her with the seeping package and gave her a peck on the cheek.

My mother took the sack into the kitchen and placed it on the butcher-block counter, where she unfolded the top and peeked inside.

"Squab," Ben said proudly, rubbing his hands together. "A dozen. Plucked, cleaned, I even took off the heads for you."

Ah. So the wetness was blood.

I glanced at my mother, whose face registered not a trace of revulsion, only delight. She was, no doubt, already doing the math, calculating the temperature and time required to crisp the skin without drying the meat and best coax forward the flavors. My mother came to life in the kitchen—it was her stage and she was the star.

"Well, I must say, this is quite the hostess gift, Ben," my mother said, laughing, appraising him with a tilt of her chin. She gave him a long look. Malabar was a tough critic. You had to earn her good opinion, a process that could take years and might not happen at all. Ben Souther, I could tell, had gone up a notch.

Ben's wife, Lily, followed close behind, bearing a bouquet of flowers from their garden in Plymouth and a bag of wild watercress, freshly picked from the banks of their stream, peppery the way Malabar loved it. About a decade older than my mother, Lily was petite and plain-pretty, with graying brown hair and a lined face that spoke of her New England practicality and utter lack of vanity.

Charles stood on the sidelines smiling broadly. He loved company, delicious meals, and stories from the past, and this weekend with his old friend Ben and Ben's wife, Lily, promised an abundance of all. I'd known the Southers since I was eight, when my mother married Charles. I knew them in the way that a child knows her parents' friends, which is to say not well and with indifference.

I was fourteen.

The cocktail hour, a sacred ritual in our home, commenced immediately. My mother and Charles each started with their usual, a tumbler of bourbon on the rocks, had a second, and then progressed to their favorite aperitif, which they called the "power pack": a dry Manhattan with a twist. The Southers followed my parents' lead, matching them drink for drink. The four of them meandered and chatted, cocktails in hand, from the living room out to the deck and then, later, across the lawn to the wooden stairs that led down to the beach. There they enjoyed the coastal abundance before them:

brackish air, a sky glowing pink with sunset, the ambient sounds of seagulls, boats on moorings, and distant waves.

My older brother, Peter, made his entrance after a long day's work as a mate on a charter fishing boat out of Wellfleet. He was sixteen, blond, and tan, his lips split from too much salt and sun. He and Ben talked striped bass—what they were eating (sand eels), where they were biting (past the bars but still close to shore). It was understood between them that this type of sport fishing, with its lowbrow chumming and high-test fishing line, was not the real deal. Ben was a fisherman's fisherman. He tied his own flies and made annual trips to Iceland and Russia to fish the world's most pristine rivers. He had already caught and released over seven hundred salmon in his lifetime, and his goal was to make it to a thousand. Still, a day on the water was a day on the water, even if it was spent with beer-guzzling tourists.

"When's dinner, Mom?" Peter asked. My brother was endlessly ravenous, always impatient.

That was all it took to get everyone back into the house. We knew what was coming next.

My mother flicked on the kitchen lights, rinsed her hands, and busied herself unwrapping the headless birds, lining them up on the countertop, and blotting their cavities dry with a fresh dishtowel. The rest of us settled onto the sturdy, high-backed stools, our elbows on the green marble counter, where we could enjoy a clear view of Malabar in action. On the enormous butcher-block island directly in front of us, aromatic herbs—basil, cilantro, thyme, oregano, mint—sprouted from a vase like a floral arrangement. A rectangle of butter had softened into a glistening mound. A giant head of garlic awaited my mother's knife. Behind us stretched our living room, framed entirely by sliding glass doors that opened onto a panoramic view of Nauset Harbor, where islands of marsh grass and sandbars were visible at low tide. Beyond the harbor was the outer beach, a strip of khaki sand punctuated by dunes that buffered us from the Atlantic Ocean. From time to time, my mother would look up from her mincing or stirring or grating, take it all in, and smile with satisfaction.

My mother had been coming to this town on Cape Cod since she was a young girl. Orleans is located at the elbow of what from the sky resembles an enormous arm pushing sixty-five miles out into the Atlantic and then flexing back toward the mainland, narrowing all the way to the curled hand of Provincetown. As a child, Malabar lived in Pochet; while married to my father, she owned a tiny cottage in Nauset Heights; and a few years ago, no doubt with some assistance from Charles, she'd bought a couple of acres of waterfront. She'd had a major renovation done when she bought this house, and it was no coincidence that the kitchen was the room with the best views.

If the idea of a woman in the kitchen calls to mind the image of a sweet homemaker in a ruffled apron or a world-weary mother dutifully fulfilling her obligation to feed her young family, you're picturing the wrong woman in the wrong kitchen. Here, at the very last house on a winding road to the bay beach, the kitchen was command central and Malabar its five-star general. Long before open kitchens were in vogue, she believed that cooks should be celebrated, not relegated to hot rooms to labor alone behind closed doors. It was in this kitchen where meringues were launched onto seas of crème anglaise, perfectly seared slabs of foie gras were drizzled with fig reductions, and salads of watercress and endive were expertly tossed with olive oil and sea salt.

My mother rarely followed recipes. She had little use for them. Hardwired to understand the chemistry of food, she needed only her palate, her instincts, and her fingertips. In a single drop of rich sauce placed on her tongue, she could detect the tiniest hint of cardamom, one lone shard of lemon zest, some whiff of a behind-the-scenes ingredient. She had an innate feel for composition and structure and how temperature might change that. She also had a keen awareness of the power of this gift, particularly where men were concerned. Armed with sharp knives, fragrant spices, and fire, my mother could create feasts whose aromas alone would entice ships full of men onto the rocks, where she would delight in watching them plunge into the abyss. I knew about the Sirens from reading Greek mythology and marveled at my mother's powers.

Candles were lit, illuminating the room, and the happy creak of corks announced that dinner was ready. Six of us assembled around the table and dug into our first course: steamed, soft-shell clams that my mother and I had plucked from a nearby sandbar at low tide earlier in the day. We pried open the shells, rolled the skin off their elongated necks, dunked the bodies into hot broth and melted butter, and popped them into our mouths. A burst of ocean.

Then came the pièce de résistance: Ben's squabs, served family-style on an enormous carving board with grooves that caught their abundant juices. Using long tongs, Malabar scooped up a tiny pigeon for each plate. Roasted to medium rare, the meat was silky and tender, fine-grained and richer than I'd expected. The skin was fatty, like a duck's, and as crisp as bacon. As accompaniment, my mother had made a savory corn pudding, some collision of kernels and eggs and cream, which she dolloped onto each plate. The flavors were complementary, sweet and salty, with a certain succulence that gave a nod to ferment.

At her first bite, my mother moaned with satisfaction. She never shied away from enjoying the fruits of her labor.

"This," Ben said, closing his eyes, "is *perfection*." Seated beside Malabar, he placed an arm around the back of her chair and raised his glass. "To the chef!"

"To Malabar," Lily seconded.

We all clinked glasses. My stepfather beamed and said, "To my sweet." Charles adored my mother, who was his second wife and nearly fifteen years his junior. They had both been married to other people when they met through friends and fell in love. Charles appreciated that my mother had stuck with him through his protracted divorce and the series of debilitating strokes he'd suffered just before their wedding that had left him partially paralyzed on his right side. He now walked with a shuffle and had learned to write and eat with his left hand.

Charles and Ben had been boyhood friends, brought together by a shared love of the town of Plymouth where Ben, a direct descendant of the *Mayflower* Pilgrims, lived and where Charles had spent summers in his youth. They were an unlikely pair—Charles always in his head, Ben so very physical—but the friendship had thrived for decades. They were within six months of each other in age, but intense and magnetic Ben seemed years younger. A hunter, a fisherman, and a conservationist—in addition to being a successful businessman—Ben had an encyclopedic knowledge of the natural world, and he shared it enthusiastically. Over dinner, I hammered him with questions: *How do horseshoe crabs mate? What causes the annual spring migration of herring? How do quahogs lay eggs?* I tried to stump him but failed. Answering questions about the environment and its inhabitants was his party trick.

As the six of us devoured our meal, Ben schooled us in pigeons, which he had been raising for more than thirty years.

"Did you know that the babies are brooded and fed by *both* parents," he said, aiming a petite drumstick my way.

"So these are, like, city pigeons?" I asked, curious if they were the same grimy creatures I knew from New York, where I was born and where my father still lived.

"Yes and no. Pigeons and doves are from the same family, Columbidae," Ben said, touching my arm as he spoke. "The birds we raise are white doves."

"Oh, the flock is so gorgeous, Rennie," Lily said. "You'll have to visit sometime and see for yourself."

"I'd love that," I said and I looked at my mother, who nodded permission.

"So how do you kill them, exactly?" Peter asked.

Ben twisted a tiny, invisible neck.

The evening went on, electric and full of small surprises. Ben was a vigorous man who spoke with his hands and explained things thoroughly but also listened intently to whoever was speaking. I noticed how his gaze kept returning to my mother throughout the meal. My mother seemed to delight in these glances, giving equine tosses of her head and laughing readily. At one point, I watched as she dragged her fork across the dome of her corn pudding. We both looked up to see if Ben was watching. He was. She shot me a furtive smile and poured me a glass of red wine. Then she poured one for Peter. "The Pinot goes perfectly with the squab," she said to us, as if we regularly paired wine with our meals.

When I looked surprised, she shrugged, amused. "If we lived in France, you would have had wine with dinner starting when you were eight!"

Ben chuckled approvingly, and my mother followed his lead with a throaty laugh.

Charles and Lily, unperturbed by my drinking, unfazed by their spouses' flirtation, erupted in laughter too.

On this night, everything was so damn funny.

At around nine o'clock, I grew restless. Even with the fans on, the dining room was uncomfortably warm, and the backs of my legs were stuck to the chair. I stole glances at the grandfather clock. *Where is he?* When the rap on the door finally came, I gave my brother a pleading glance. He didn't budge from his seat.

Please, I begged Peter with my eyebrows raised. *Come on. Just do this.*

Peter rolled his eyes and shrugged halfheartedly but then gave in and went to the door.

"Can I be excused?" I asked my mother. "I need some fresh air."

She nodded, barely registering the request.

As I stood to clear my plate, I felt tipsy from the wine. I sped upstairs, brushed my teeth and hair, and rushed to the door, slowing down as I neared it to appear composed.

My brother and our neighbor Ted were standing on the front porch, shooting the breeze. We all knew the drill: Peter said good night and eased back inside, and Ted and I drifted around the house and down the wooden steps to the shore below. We didn't have much to say to each other, this boy and I, so we didn't talk. We went to our usual spot, lay down on the coarse sand, and started to make out as we'd been doing every night for almost a week.

A couple walked past us, hand in hand, unaware of our presence on the sand behind them, and settled in against a rock near the water's edge to admire the moon's reflection on the inlet. We usually pulled apart when someone intruded, but this time Ted put a finger to his lips, telling me to stay quiet, and then, with a tug, jerked my tank top up and over my breasts. I lay flat on the sand, stunned by this unexpected maneuver. Ted's grinning face, illuminated by the bright moonlight, was full of adolescent lust and greed. His eyes feasted on my chest. Dark blond hair peeked out from his armpits, and the muscles in his shoulders twitched. Then he started—first one breast and then the other, squeezing and releasing, causing sparks to flare in my chest and a warmth to gather between my legs.

By the time I returned home, my mother's dinner party was winding down. Lily was clearing the dessert plates, and my stepfather looked exhausted. Even Ben and my mother seemed subdued. I slipped past unnoticed and went upstairs.

I crawled into bed, and my encounter with Ted started looping through my head. I couldn't stop thinking about what he'd done. The rules of teenage sexual engagement were unambiguous —there was no going back. I knew that a new starting line had been drawn and the next time we sneaked off together, my exposed breasts would be understood as a given.

The curtains in my bedroom were open, the windows cranked as wide as they could possibly go, and even so, it was sweltering. My hair, damp with the humid salt air, stuck to my neck, and the thread-bare cotton sheets, gritty with sand, clung to my legs. The moon was the only thing that looked cool, like a cold piece of metal that I wanted to press against my face. Outside, there wasn't even the slightest breeze to tug the fishing boats against their moorings or disturb my mother's wind chimes. The house was silent too. My parents and their guests must have finally gone to bed.

So much had changed in my body over the past year. I used to have to chase boys to get their attention. Now all I had to do around them was hang on to our porch railing and arch away from it, push my toes into the soft sand, or lift my eyes, squinting as if into the sun, and they were rapt. After a long spell of stillness, my body had burst — breasts erupting, hips expanding, skin stretched taut over new horizons of flesh. My insides had gone wild too.

I cramped and bled each month, but no one had told me about the rest of it: how dank and loamy it was in there, how even when I didn't have my period, so much was going on, shifting and soft-ening, leaving slippery clues for me to follow. As I floated toward sleep, I dreamily replayed the night's events again and again — shirt up, hands on breasts — until an utterly new commotion un-leashed itself inside me. An unfamiliar wave swelled from a center deep within and ricocheted through me, licking every nerve and cell along the way.

What just happened?

I felt fully awake again, trying to figure out the steps I had taken, wanting to memorize the path to this extraordinary place, but it eluded me. I drifted in and out of a fitful sleep.

"Wake up, Rennie."

I felt a hand on my shoulder and pulled the sheet over my head.

"Rennie, please."

Even before I turned and saw her face, I could hear a peculiar quaver in my mother's whisper and smell the remnants of the Pinot Noir. Her voice sounded hesitant and desperate. The mattress sank where she lowered herself beside me, and my body stiffened against the depression. I kept my eyes shut and steadied my exhalations.

"Rennie!" The whisper, more urgent now, still held an unfamiliar tremor. She pulled down the sheet. "Please wake up."

Even with her beside me, hovering over me, her breath warm against my ear, I didn't want to abandon thoughts of Ted. Why was my mother in my room in the middle of the night? For a moment, I panicked: Did she have some sixth sense that I'd just made my first foray into sex? Or had Peter betrayed me and told her that I'd been sneaking off, getting into trouble? I turned away from her, half asleep, in no mood for a lecture. Still floating from the sensation of what had just happened, I didn't want to lose track of it.

"Rennie, wake up. Please wake up."

Just go away, I thought.

"Sweetheart. Please. I need you."

At this, I opened my eyes. Malabar was in her nightgown, her hair mussed. I sat up.

"Mom, what's wrong? Is everything okay?"

"Ben Souther just kissed me."

I took in this information. Tried to make sense of it. Couldn't. I rubbed my eyes. My mother was still there beside me.

"Ben kissed me," my mother repeated.

A noun, a verb, an object — such a simple sentence, really, and yet I couldn't comprehend it. Why would Ben Souther kiss my mother? It wasn't that I was naive; I knew that people kissed people they weren't supposed to. My parents had not shielded me from stories of both of their transgressions during their marriage, and in this way, I knew more about infidelity than most children. I was four when my parents broke up, six when my father remarried, seven when that new marriage started to fall apart, and eight when my mother was finally able to wed Charles, who'd been separated from but still married to his first wife when they met.

Ben was married, too, of course, to Lily. The Southers had been married for thirty-five years.

Mom and Charles. Ben and Lily.

The four of them had been couple-friends for as long as my mother and stepfather had known each other, about a decade now.

That's what really stumped me about the kiss — the friendship between Ben and Charles. The two men adored each other. Their affection went back some fifty years, maybe more, to a time when they were young enough to skip stones across the flat, gray water of Plymouth Bay, where they pretended to be Pilgrims and built forts in the dunes, fending off imaginary enemies with stick muskets. Over the years, they'd hunted and fished together, dated each other's sisters, been ushers at each other's weddings, and become godfathers to each other's sons.

"What do you mean, Ben kissed you?" Suddenly I was fully awake. I pictured her slapping him in response. That was something my mother might do. "What happened?"

"We took a walk after dinner, just the two of us, and he pulled me into him, like this." My mother crossed her arms around herself, simultaneously demonstrating Ben's caress and embracing its memory. Then she collapsed the rest of the way onto the bed, smiling, and stretched out alongside me.

Apparently, there had been no slap.

"I still can't believe it. Ben Souther kissed me," she said.

What was it about her voice tonight?

"He kissed me, Rennie."

There it was again: joy. A tone I hadn't heard from her since before Charles's strokes. Joy had fallen from the night sky and landed in my mother's voice. One kiss — the gleam and shine of it, what it might portend — had changed everything.

"He wants me to meet him in New York next week. He has a board meeting — some salmon thing — and Lily plans to stay in Plymouth. I don't know what to do."

We were lying on our backs, heat emanating from our bodies. "What do you think I should do?"

We both knew this was a rhetorical question. Malabar was a planner. She had already made up her mind.

"I'm going to need your help, sweetie," she said. "I need to figure out how to do this. How to make this possible."

I lay as still as a corpse, unsure of what to say.

"Of course, I don't want to hurt Charles. I'd rather die than cause him more grief. That's my top priority. Charles must never find out. He would be devastated." She paused as if to consider Charles one last time and then rolled onto her side to face me. "You have to help me, Rennie."

My mother needed me. I knew I was supposed to fill the space in the conversation, but the words weren't coming. I didn't know what to say.

"Aren't you happy for me, Rennie?" my mother asked, rising onto an elbow.

I looked at her face and into her eyes, dark and dewy with hope, and all at once, I was happy for her. And for me. Malabar was falling in love and she'd picked me as her confidante, a role I hadn't realized I'd longed for until that moment. Perhaps this could be a good thing. Maybe someone as vital as Ben could startle my mother out of the malaise she'd been in since Charles's strokes and that had appeared, at times, in the years before. Perhaps in the fall, when school started, my mother would get dressed for carpool. No more coat over her nightgown or sheet marks on her puffy morning face. Maybe she'd brush her hair, smear some gloss across her lips, and greet the children on our route with a cheery "Hello" like all of the other mothers.

"Of course I'm happy," I said. "I'm so happy for you."

Her reaction — grateful tears — emboldened me.

"After all you've been through, you deserve this," I told her.

"Sweetie, you can't tell anyone. Not a soul. Not your brother, not your father, not your friends. No one. This is serious. Promise me that, Rennie. You must take this secret to your grave."

I promised immediately, thrilled to have landed a starring role in my mother's drama, oblivious to the fact that I was being out-maneuvered for the second time that night.

The people who occupied the bedrooms around us — my brother; my stepfather; Ben and his wife, Lily — were all peacefully asleep. They had no idea that the ground beneath them had shifted. My mother had narrowed her vision and chosen happiness, and I had willingly signed on, both of us ignoring the dangers of the new terrain.

When dawn spilled through my open windows and the sun climbed up and over the outer beach, that long spit of sand and dunes that separates our inlet from the Atlantic, the sky turned a brilliant fuchsia streaked with red. I awoke full of hope and no longer thinking about Ted. I already knew that when he showed up on our porch that evening, I would not sneak down to the beach to feel the determined pressure of his pelvis against mine. Instead, I would stay home and bear witness to my mother's seduction.

TWO

IF WE ARE to believe that a butterfly flapping its wings in South America can stir up a storm in Texas, what might be the unruly consequences of an illicit kiss on a country road? This marked the beginning of the rest of my life. Once I chose to follow my mother, there was no turning back. I became her protector and sentinel, always on the lookout for what might give her away.

I awoke fizzy with elation, buoyed by the joy in my mother's voice, still drunk on the intimacy of our exchange. Malabar had chosen me, and my body vibrated with an ineffable sense of opportunity.

My brother was already in the kitchen, hunched over a bowl of cereal, when I floated downstairs. Along the counter, half-empty glasses held the stale aroma of last night's wine. Peter had turned sixteen in June, had a separate apartment over the garage (a source of envy), owned his own boat (another), and already had an eye toward the person he planned to become.

"You know that Ted is a total creep, right, Ren?" Peter said, shoveling in a spoonful of flakes. He backhanded a drop of milk from the corner of his mouth.

I blushed, flashing to Ted pulling up my top. Yes, I did realize that

Ted was a creep. He was the kind of kid who, five years earlier, had spent summer evenings catching frogs, putting firecrackers in their mouths, then laughing wildly when their legs went flying.

"No, he's a good guy," I said to my brother, the words as smooth as marbles. Even though I was no longer interested in Ted, admitting that he was a jerk was not an option. In our family, being right trumped being truthful. There was no room for uncertainty, so you never let down your guard.

Peter smirked at this unlikelihood and nudged his bowl toward the sink side of the counter.

Since our parents' divorce, a decade earlier, it had been the three of us: Mom, Peter, me. My father was on the sidelines, of course, occupying the every-other-weekend-and-alternating-holidays real estate, and my stepfather, Charles, was present, too, with his four grown children from his previous marriage, now my stepsiblings. But our fundamental family unit since the divorce had always been a triangle, that sturdy shape. Except on this morning, our geometry was changing. Before the end of the day, Peter's side would be cut loose, and once untethered from him, my mother and I would shape-shift into a single straight line, the most direct conduit for her secret.

—

"Good morning," Malabar sang out, addressing no one in particular. She breezed into the kitchen wearing a cotton robe loosely belted over a sheer nightgown; her hair was tousled. It was a bit cooler this morning but still humid, and the sky, a swirl of purple-gray, promised the relief of rain. At the window on the far side of the kitchen, my mother caught her reflection and pursed her lips. In the cold light of day, she eyed the age spots scattered on her hands and the slack skin at the base of her neck, a nectarine a few days past perfect.

Still, she was lovely, slim and strong with shiny auburn hair that framed an alluring face with a dimple high on her left cheek, a mark left by forceps that was a reminder of her tough entry into this world. Although she cultivated an air of elegant aloofness, she was surprisingly game, willing to bait hooks and often the first to dive into rough waves. I know now that she'd lost some essential piece of herself when she gave up her career as a journalist in New York City and opted for a gentler life and financial security by marrying Charles, who had family wealth. According to my father, my grandmother often told Malabar, "You marry one man to have your children and another to take care of you in your old age." But if that had been my mother's intention, subconscious or otherwise, in marrying Charles, it was not working out as planned. Charles had made my mother wealthy, but she was doing the lion's share of caregiving. Malabar would be forty-nine in the fall and no doubt felt despair over the unexpected changes in her life.

She raised her chin defiantly against her reflection, turned, and fixed on me a look that proved I hadn't dreamed the previous night's encounter.

"Young lady," she said, arching an eyebrow, "you and I have things to discuss later."

Peter shook his head, wondering what I'd done this time. I figured he thought I'd been caught canoodling with Ted, but he mimed a quick toke on a spliff. *That it?* His eyes twinkled.

Then my mother made her tea, an elaborate ritual to clear the previous night's fog — brought on by cocktails, wine, a sleeping pill or two — and usher in the new day. She dumped the kettle, filled it with fresh water, and set it on the stove. As it warmed, she pried off the lid of a tin of Lapsang souchong, and, *poof,* the room filled with its distinctive smoky aroma. With her thumb and forefinger, she felt for the perfect amount of dried leaves, which, pinch by pinch, she sprinkled into her teapot. When at last the kettle sputtered and whistled, hot water met leaves, and the tea was left to steep under an outlandish rooster-shaped cozy.

Charles shuffled in next, freshly showered, all aristocratic square jaw, thick horn-rimmed glasses, and slicked-back gray hair. He looked as he had since his strokes six years earlier: resigned to the fact that he was no longer calling the shots. Revered as the visionary behind Plimoth Plantation,* the living-history museum he'd founded years earlier and to which he remained passionately devoted, Charles was captivated by various archaeological enthusiasms. His latest obsession was finding the wreck of a long-lost pirate ship called the *Whydah Gally*. What I admired most about Charles was how fundamentally different he was from my parents—he didn't swear or lose his temper, and he had no problem conceding a point. Well-mannered, quietly formal, and genial, Charles longed for little more than a good book, preferably history, read anywhere but on the beach. He announced this desire by praying to the rain god every summer morning. "Please, dear rain god," he would intone over breakfast, "do your thing so I won't have to sit on that hot, sandy beach." This always made us all laugh.

"Looks like you'll have your way today, Charles," Peter said, and our stepfather smiled, appreciating the ominous sky.

"We could drive up to Wellfleet and see what Barry Clifford is up to," Charles suggested to no one in particular. Barry Clifford, known locally as Cape Cod's Indiana Jones, was on the hunt for sunken treasures and, like Charles, had set his sights on finding the *Whydah*.

No one bit.

Normally, as my mother sipped her tea, she would serve Charles his morning brew: a spoonful of Sanka in a mug, the remains of her boiling water, a single brisk stir. This was his preference, my mother assured us, a habit left over from his bachelor days. But this morning, with Ben and Lily visiting for the weekend, my mother made a pot of coffee with freshly ground beans, and as I watched Charles drink it down with relish, I wondered if he truly did prefer Sanka.

We sat in our usual places along the counter, Charles, Peter, and

---

* The living-history museum Plimoth Plantation takes its spelling of *Plymouth* from the historical account of the town written by Governor William Bradford.

me, all of us looking into the kitchen, where my mother, peppy now from her tea, glided from stove to island to sink to refrigerator, readying breakfast. She had decided on homemade corn fritters, and she was bullying fresh egg whites into stiff peaks, shaving corn from ears, grating nutmeg. Butter softened on the counter, and maple syrup warmed over a low heat on the stove.

Ben and Lily were the last to appear, freshly showered, hair combed, Lily's graying locks held in place with a bright yellow headband. She wasn't the kind of woman to fork over money to a fancy salon. Lily sported Bermuda shorts, a polo shirt, and a pair of reading glasses that rode precariously low on her nose. Under her arm was a weighty tome on the history of Norway; she held it up for my stepfather's approval, and Charles gave her a nod and smile.

Ben greeted Charles with his energetic "How do!," then strode into our kitchen, took both my mother's hands in his, and, in full view of his wife and my stepfather, kissed her right on the mouth.

"Malabar," he said, his face close enough to hers that he could see her pupils expand, "that might have been the best damn dinner of my entire life!"

"Ben," Lily said, playfully scolding her husband, "leave that poor woman alone." Her voice was thin and raspy, the aftereffects of cancer treatments that she'd had in her twenties. Radiation seeds had been planted in her chest, and though the radiation had successfully halted the tumor's growth, it went on to ravage other parts of her body: her ovaries, her heart, and, now, her vocal cords. Although she was no longer sick, you had only to look at Lily to know that she wasn't well either. *Frail* was the word that came to mind.

"Out of the question," replied Ben, who neither dropped my mother's hands nor took his eyes off her. "How many women know what to do when you give them a bag of fresh squab?" He shook his head in disbelief at his good fortune. "Marvelous. Just marvelous."

A happy heat spread over my mother's face. Was there relief in there too? Had she second-guessed what had happened the night before, tried to convince herself that the kiss was nothing more than a drunken pass to be forgotten in the morning light? If so, now she could be sure that wasn't the case. Ben Souther had just publicly declared her marvelous, and that act had awakened the dormant marvelousness within her.

My mother wriggled her hands free and grabbed a large fork, the kind used to skewer meat on a grill. "Ben Souther, get out of my kitchen this instant!"

Ben laughed as he backed out, his hands raised in surrender. He took his place on the other side of the counter, on the stool beside my stepfather. Ben's hands chopped wood, built fences, deftly killed animals of every sort. Charles's hands were baby-soft, his right one lacking dexterity since his strokes. Seeming to bask in his oldest friend's admiration of his wife, my stepfather patted a palsied fist on Ben's back, his bones showing through the papery skin. (My four stepsiblings could never quite decide if my mother was a gold digger, after the family money, or someone worth her weight in gold for staying with Charles after his strokes.)

Outside, gulls were aloft, suspended like mobiles on the wind until something shifted and forced them to veer off in search of the next ethereal gust. Goldfinches and chickadees flitted to the feeder and jousted for the last mouthfuls of seeds before the rain began, and a lone chipmunk, beneath the fray, collected the spoils. The light was beautiful and then suddenly gone, in its place electricity.

As if on cue, my mother lowered two gorgeous stacks of corn fritters, crisped to golden-brown perfection and topped with thick slices of bacon, onto the counter. As the plates clinked on the marble, Charles and Ben bowed their heads in unison, inhaling the holy communion of maple syrup and pork.

—

After breakfast, I went upstairs to document the monumental happenings of the previous twenty-four hours — my first orgasm and my mother's illicit kiss. Although I had long kept a journal, until this morning, the contents hadn't been particularly engrossing. Overnight, my life had become something else entirely. I wrote for hours.

When I finally returned downstairs, I saw that my mother needed my counsel. At a loss for how to move the game along with Ben, she solicited my help. *What do I do?* she mouthed. Outside, it was pouring, and inside, the grownups lounged listlessly, reading books and watching a tennis match.

She and I flitted from nook to nook, my mother telling me secrets that must have been a great relief for her to confess. In the window seat in her bedroom, she admitted that she'd been depressed for years. Had I known this? she asked. I knew she often had a hard time getting out of bed and that I had to beg her to brush the back of her hair, an unruly nest, for carpool. But like most children, I was self-absorbed, worried about my own friendships and crushes, and I hadn't been overly preoccupied with my mother's interior life. All I really wanted was to be assured that she loved me more than anyone else.

In the pantry, amid bottles of olive oil and cooking paraphernalia, Malabar confessed that after Charles's strokes, she'd felt she had no choice but to marry him. "Before he got sick, I'd never been so in love in all my life," she told me. "But none of the doctors could tell me if he'd ever be the same. He couldn't talk. They didn't know if he'd regain all his mental faculties, let alone his physical ones. He'd been so good to me and to you and Peter," she said, and she suddenly embraced me.

Our lives would have been so different had my mother not married Charles. We'd still be in our old apartment on the Upper East Side of Manhattan, spending summers in our tiny Cape cottage in Nauset Heights, where Peter and I shared a bedroom that my mother had to walk through to get to her own even smaller room. I've never been privy to my mother's finances — to this day, they are a mystery to me — but I can't imagine that she could have bought and renovated the large house we were in right now were it not for Charles's assistance.

"Besides," she said, "we were already engaged." She picked at a hangnail on her ring finger until it bled. "Going ahead with the marriage was the only decent thing to do."

That was the first time I understood that she'd considered other options. Later, she took my hands, averted her eyes as if holding on to some lingering sense of maternal propriety, and said, "Rennie, Charles has been more child than husband since his strokes. If you get my meaning."

I did.

At various times during that day and during the weeks, months, and years to come, my brother, Peter, would walk by and see us in solemn discussion. He would slow, waiting for an invitation from one of us to join in these conspicuous conversations. It had always been us three, after all. Before Ben's kiss, Peter's opinion was as valued as mine. But now our mother would abruptly stop talking and regard her son with impatience and a look that said, *Is there something you need?* The sting of rejection would cross Peter's face — easier for me to remember now than to see at the time — and he would move on.

"What's up with you two?" he asked us on that first day when my mother and I were cloistered in the pantry. He hated being excluded.

"Oh, it's nothing, really," I assured him. "Boy problems. Trust me, you'd be bored." Perhaps Peter would think I was confiding in my mother about Ted.

From here on out, I would be lying to everyone.

———

The sun finally pushed through the sky in broad columns of slanted light. The tide was dead low, that still hour that marks the sea's withdrawal and illuminates the teeming life beneath the surface of our bay: moon snails pushing plow-like across the sandy bottom, horseshoe crabs coupling, schools of minnows moving in perfect synchronicity. As the procession of sunbeams merged into one, the day became long with light, and a space in my mind opened like that between a boat and a dock.

I grabbed a wire bucket that we kept in the outdoor shower, opened one of the sliding glass doors, and stuck my head inside. "Who wants to go clamming?" I asked.

Lily and Charles looked up from their books, smiled lazily, and demurred. But Ben rose quickly, as I knew he would, eager to be active. The man could not sit still for long. My mother regarded me with more gratitude than I'd thought possible but remained in her chair. She would need, I understood, public convincing.

Did it occur to me then that I was betraying Charles, who had always been gentle and kind to Peter and me and whom I loved? If it did, I pushed the thought away. All I knew at that moment was I felt lucky. My mother had chosen me, and, together, we were embarking on a great adventure.

"Come on, Mom," I pressed. "It'll be fun."

And, as in a game of chess, having moved a piece and let it go, I could never undo the move.

—

Out in the marshes, across the bay and past rippled deserts of sand flats, noisy black-capped terns squawked disapprovingly at our arrival. Mom, Ben, and I slipped into a pond as warm as a bath and sank into the silt. The water was only waist-deep, but we bent our knees as if sitting on imaginary chairs and submerged to our chins. We clouded the water as we shuffled, trying to coax the blunt instruments of our feet to behave like eyes and hands, feeling for lumps in the dark mud. But even in these still waters, surprises lurked below; eels slithered along thighs, minnows bumped ankles, spiny creatures crawled over bare feet. Before long a crab scuttled up my mother's leg and she sought protection in Ben's lap, where I pictured his arms, invisible beneath the black water, wrapped around her midriff.

I left the pond, claiming to know of a better spot — there was always a better pond just beyond the one you were in — and dashed across the prickly marsh grass, forgetting my bucket as I fled. There, in the next hole, I found my rhythm, greeting clam after clam with my feet. I turned up my oversize T-shirt to create a pouch and placed the cherrystones and littlenecks in it until my shirt was blackened with mud and stretched long.

Perhaps an hour went by, maybe not quite. The sun was sinking in the late-afternoon sky and an incoming tide ushered cool water into the marsh. I was cold. I made my way back to the boat, scrubbed my catch in the sand, and piled the clean clams in shallow water, where innumerable trails rippled across the bay's floor. Snails, their paths lingering ghosts of their journey. As the ocean washed over the clams, I watched their hinged shells part and the pink curve of their flesh emerge for a final sip.

In the distance, my mother had also emerged and was sitting on the bank of the pool, long-necked and confident, her skin gleaming. She was flirting with Ben, who was covered in marsh mud and seemed to be pretending to be a creature from the deep. At last he hauled himself out alongside her, animal-like, on all fours, and their body language abruptly changed. They dipped their heads together, and, even from far off, I could tell that they were whispering, making sure their words did not take flight across the bay.

Were they making a decision right then and there? Choosing whether or not to proceed? Having kissed, they could never not have kissed. Could that be their rationale? *We've already done this thing . . .*

I wonder now if either of them was arguing against embarking on their affair, bringing up the cons, the repercussions, the friendships and families at stake.

When Ben stood and pulled Malabar to her feet, the slight tilt of my mother's head, her incline toward him, made it clear that they'd decided to go ahead with it, as casually and permanently as if they had tossed a stone into the ocean.

THREE

Ever since my parents split up, when I was five, my mother had been chasing a new and better life. That was in the early 1970s, a time when the national divorce rate was soaring. First my father moved out and I saw him less frequently, every other weekend and on alternating Wednesday nights. He remarried in 1971. Then my mother followed suit, remarrying in 1974. Back then, children were tossed into new families and cities and schools, and expected to adapt, which is what happened to me as I entered the fourth grade.

Peter and I were nine and eight, respectively, when our mother married Charles and we moved from a modest apartment in Manhattan, where we'd shared a bedroom, into the Greenwood family estate in Chestnut Hill, Massachusetts, an affluent suburb of Boston. Overnight, my brother and I acquired four adult stepsiblings — none of whom lived with us — and vaulted up several rungs on the socioeconomic ladder.

Our new home was a mansion with seventeen bedrooms, nine bathrooms, a library, formal living and dining rooms, a grand entrance hall over which swung two table-size chandeliers, and a servants' wing twice the size of our old apartment. Some of the rooms seemed almost as big as tennis courts, long enough for me to do my favorite tumbling pass—run, cartwheel, back walkover—and came with fort-size fireplaces. Our new silverware, from Charles's mother's side, was heavier than our old, its weight suggesting something I couldn't quite grasp. My stepsiblings warned me of bats and the ghost of a long-dead gardener who haunted the grounds.

I felt ill at ease in this place, which we referred to by its address: 100 Essex. I missed my father and my friends in New York City as well as the company of my brother, who was no longer my roommate. Peter's bedroom was far away from mine, on a different floor and wing; we didn't even have a staircase in common for random collisions. In the new house, that classic adage "Children should be seen and not heard" was taken even farther—children were neither seen *nor* heard. But the first time I saw my mother descend the splendid marble staircase, the one that curved like the tip of Cape Cod itself, it was clear that she was in her element.

Every other weekend, Peter and I were shuttled off to visit our father, usually at his cabin in Newtown, Connecticut, which had been our family's weekend getaway place when we all lived together in Manhattan. We would take a Greyhound bus from Boston to Hartford and sit directly behind the driver, our de facto babysitter, who'd been informed by our mother that we were traveling alone. My father would be waiting for us at the station, and he'd drive us the rest of the way. The tiny white house sat on a plateau in the forest ringed by toppled stone walls and towering tulip trees. Charming and barebones, the cabin was in every way the opposite of the mansion we now called home. There was a dilapidated outhouse to the rear, an antique Franklin stove in the main room that kept us toasty on chilly nights, and an old steel tub that my father filled with heated water on the rare occasions when we bathed there.

Our weekends at the cabin followed a routine: We cooked pasta with meat sauce on Friday night, went trout fishing in the stream behind the house the next morning, and invited the neighbors down for supper on Saturday—always steak, grilled rare over an open fire. Occasionally, my father had a female companion, but the lack of indoor plumbing discouraged all but the most stalwart of girl-friends. Midday on Sunday, back to Chestnut Hill we went. Usually we took the bus, but every once in a while my father drove us, his mood darkening as we crossed the state line into Massachusetts and getting incrementally worse the closer we got to 100 Essex. At the final right-hand turn down the long drive that led to the house, he would eye the odometer and tell us the exact number of miles he'd traveled to take us home.

The prevailing wisdom concerning divorce at the time was that children were resilient creatures who would fare better with happy parents. This was the new paradigm, or at least it was the version of it that our parents embraced and that we helped spin. (Today we understand that what's best for the parents is not necessarily best for the children.) On top of my mother's desk, frozen in a 1970s acrylic-cube frame, are six photos of Peter and me taken during this period. In every shot, our eyes look vacant and our expressions ra-diate worry and loss.

—

To this day, I cannot imagine my parents ever having been in love, nor can I fathom what attracted them to each other. Although there are photographs of them together in our baby albums, I have no memories of them as a married couple. My father wrote daily, loved to fish and garden, and was content to live within his means. My mother was insatiable and acquisitive, always striving for a better, more fabulous life. To me, my parents have always seemed like po-lar opposites.

My mother is well into her eighties now and suffers from de-mentia, but she remains as grand as her impossibly formidable first name. When asked about its origins, she explained that while she was born in Malabar Hill in Bombay, she was actually named after the fictional Malabar Caves in E. M. Forster's classic *A Passage to*

India—the literary distinction was important to her. Only she got it wrong; the caves in Forster's novel are the Marabar Caves. That part of her story remains a mystery to me, but perhaps she related to what the caves represented: the loneliness of human existence.

I imagine her on the first day of kindergarten sitting cross-legged alongside the other five-year-olds as they went around the circle introducing themselves— "Ruth," "Elizabeth," "Rachel," and then, at her turn, that mouthful of a name: "Malabar." Would she have become the same all-powerful person she did had she been named Betty or Jane? I wonder about this. As any magician knows, it is not the smoke and mirrors that trick people; it is that the human mind makes assumptions and misunderstands them as truths.

Born in Bombay, India, in 1931, Malabar was the only child of Bert and Vivian, two charismatic and narcissistic people whose epic and alcohol-fueled relationship resulted in their being twice married to and twice divorced from each other. A few months after Malabar— "Mabby" to her parents—was born, her mother, desperately sick with a tapeworm, discovered that her compulsively cheating husband was up to his usual tricks. She took her newborn daughter, fled India, and returned to her home in New York City.

My mother's first memory of her father—her first memory *period*—was opening the door to her mother's bedroom one morning when she was about three and seeing his penis. "I'm your father, Mabby," Bert announced, as if this explained everything—his being in their New York apartment, his erect penis, his existence. Her father, apparently trying to save his marriage, was on leave from India. This was the protocol of his firm: three years abroad, three months home.

The reconciliation didn't work. Malabar remembers an extended trip with her mother when she was about five, and records confirm that Vivian traveled to California in 1935. From there, Malabar dimly recalls their long drive to Nevada, the only state at the time that offered multiple grounds for divorce and required no waiting period or proof of residency.

But my volatile and charismatic grandparents couldn't stay away from each other, and their first divorce didn't stick. In a grand second marriage proposal, Bert got down on bended knee to declare, yet again, his undying love for Vivian, this time at a Christmas dinner party in front of a handful of close friends. He presented her with an extraordinary gift: a necklace of diamonds, rubies, emeralds, and other gems that she had seen and coveted on her last trip to India but never imagined she could own. Stunned by my grandfather's extravagance and generosity, my grandmother accepted his proposal, and the two remarried in 1940. A year later, my grandfather secretly sired a son with a woman he promised to marry.

My grandparents split permanently after my mother finished high school, and Malabar ended up with the necklace. Over the years, this dubious trophy of Bert and Vivian's doomed relationship took hold of my mother's imagination. What it represented to her exactly, I'll never know—the Raj, the glamour of another era, her parents' love?—but I suspect that, deep down, it symbolized the life she yearned for and thought she deserved.

Malabar grew up, went to Radcliffe College, and began a career in journalism in New York City, where she worked first as a reporter at *American Heritage* and then as a staff writer at Time-Life Books. With a nudge from a psychiatrist who was helping her with commitment issues—unwed at twenty-eight, she was considered a spinster—she embarked on a marriage with my father, Paul Brodeur, who was then a staff writer for the Talk of the Town in the *New Yorker*.

My parents' life together began promisingly. Their first child, Christopher, was born on October 15, 1961, and as their small family grew, so did their respective careers. My mother's articles and my father's stories were getting published. They were young and ambitious. Then, in early 1964, when my mother was pregnant with her second child, tragedy struck. Christopher choked on a piece of meat he'd hidden in his cheek as the family drove back to the city from the cabin in Newtown. My brother was two and a half years old when he died.

Peter had no choice but to marinate in Malabar's grief until his birth in June. Then, sixteen months after Peter, I came into the world. I was born on Christopher's birthday, October 15. My birth has always felt like the result of a powerful and subconscious maternal urge to replace the life that had been lost.

As a young child, I intuited something inexplicably awry about my birthday. Long before our parents told Peter and me about Christopher's existence and tragic death, I understood that a little boy had been part of our family but no longer was. Clues abounded. A tiny pair of moss-green lederhosen, neither Peter's nor mine, hung from a hook on our bedroom door in the cabin; a blue-jean-clad teddy bear that we were not allowed to touch sat on a windowsill in my mother's bedroom. There were photographs of a smiling child wearing my mother's sunglasses and fake-smoking my father's pipe. He was a brown-eyed version of Peter and me.

When I asked my father's mother, an apple-cheeked, born-again Christian, questions about the boy in the photographs, she told me about sin, about who got into heaven and who got sent to hell and why. The concept boggled my mind. My parents had never taken me to church, and I didn't know about Jesus, let alone that I should accept Him as my Savior.

But what about the boy? I wanted to know. He looked like Peter and me. Where was he?

Her answer? Purgatory.

My takeaway, undoubtedly not my grandmother's intent, was that I was a sinner, as were my parents, and Christopher's death was connected to our collective trespasses. Why else would God play such a trick with my birthday? It also occurred to me that Christopher, wherever he was, must be none too pleased with my trying to replace him.

—

"Who do you love most in the world?"

This was the essential question of my childhood and one that I asked my mother almost daily, usually as she put on her makeup. We'd be in her dressing room, me on the bed, my mother perched on a cushioned stool in front of a skirted dressing table, a tube of frosted-pink lipstick at the ready, her pretty face illuminated by a multisided makeup mirror. Every time, she would appear to ponder my question.

Please say me. Please say me.

Malabar's favorite was a constantly shifting point on her compass. My mother would take her time before answering, applying a perfect coat of lipstick, and then surprise me with a sudden embrace and a conspiratorial whisper: "You, my silly girl. You." God, I adored having her full attention, being wrapped in her arms and reassured. But love *was* conditional with Malabar. If I'd disappointed her in some way, had acted selfishly or broken an unspoken rule, she would stay silent, allowing me to feel the full weight of her abandonment and the possibility that she loved Peter or Christopher more than me.

Prone to melancholy, my mother used to recite a poem to me called "Monday's Child," always slowing down when she reached the final lines.

Monday's child is fair of face
Tuesday's child is full of grace
Wednesday's child is full of woe
Thursday's child has far to go
Friday's child is loving and giving
Saturday's child works hard for a living

And the child that is born on the Sabbath day
Is bonny and blithe and good and gay.

I came to understand why her eyes got misty. Peter and I had been born on ordinary days, but Christopher was Sunday's child, the most special of all. He'd been her cherished firstborn, a boy whose birthday I had unwittingly hijacked. Christopher became my obsession, but there was no competing with a ghost. I couldn't help but think that if my parents had been given their choice between Christopher and me, they would have picked him.

As children, Peter and I got the story of our brother's death bit by bit from various sources, and, as happens, the facts changed in the telling. Christopher had stashed a piece of meat inside his cheek, that much we knew. No one was aware he'd hidden the meat. Everyone knew he'd hidden the meat. Christopher started to choke when the car hit a bump in the road. The choking started in the parking lot of an antique store. Our parents were with him at the time. Our parents were in the store, but the au pair ran to get them. A fireman tried to resuscitate him. A doctor, who had an office next door, refused to help. Our father felt responsible, according to our mother. Our mother felt responsible, according to our father. The au pair *was* responsible, according to our aunt. It was God's will, our grandmother declared.

But nothing changed the outcome — our older brother had died before Peter and I were born, and we would always live in his shadow.

I have known my mother only as the person she became after Christopher died: a mother who had lost a child. Who might she have been before? I imagine her, in the days and weeks and months that followed Christopher's death, engaging in magical thinking, as the grief-stricken do. I picture her daily shock on waking up after a few hours of respite, thanks to her sleeping pills, and remembering again that her son was dead. Forgetting and remembering. I wonder if that part of it is over for her now, if five and a half decades is long enough to metabolize such a loss or if there are still moments when time collapses and her agony overtakes everything.

—

Whenever Malabar got sentimental, she would pull out the Indian necklace. She would retrieve the purple velvet case from the depths of her walk-in closet, place it on her bed between us, and pop open the lid. There it was.

"This necklace is the most valuable item I own. Do you understand, Rennie? It's extraordinary and priceless, absolutely priceless," she would say. "I should leave it to a museum. It would be irresponsible to do anything else."

Then Malabar would make me promise, again and again, that if she left the necklace to me, I would never sell it, no matter what. I swore on my life that I wouldn't.

On one occasion, she wrapped the sparkling collar around my neck and I felt the mighty weight of it, our yoke. I might have been ten at the time, no longer a towhead but still with light blond hair, almost invisible eyebrows, and round, childish features. Everything about me was soft—my nose, my cheeks, my jawline—and I lacked the essential gravitas for the piece. My mother, dark-haired, dark-eyed, fiercely beautiful, laughed. We both did. I looked ridiculous.

"Don't worry. You'll grow into it," she said, unclasping it. "You shall wear it on your wedding day." Then she lovingly placed the necklace back in its box.

FOUR

To cover for Malabar's affair, I would tell Charles one thing, my father and Peter another, my friends something else, attempting to explain either my mother's absences or my own. Someone had to take care of Charles when she was gone. He still went to the office every day but required assistance at home. With his right side paralyzed and his weak heart, my stepfather needed help preparing dinner and uncapping his bottle of nitroglycerin pills, those tiny white dots of relief that he popped into his mouth at least a dozen times a day. I learned to make excuses and bury the truth with whatever I could throw at it.

Lying wasn't wholly new to me. It comes with the territory when your parents get divorced and the two people you love and need most become adversaries. When I saw something disturbing at one parent's house—an overnight guest or a dozen pills on the bedside table—I knew better than to seek comfort from the other because that bit of information would be used as ammunition in their warfare.

What's more, lying and stealing were never truly discouraged in my home. The taking of "small liberties" to ensure that my mother got what she wanted in every situation was routine and often great fun, usually part and parcel of some elaborate game Malabar devised for our family's amusement. There was our annual raid of the Millers' vineyard to filch grapes for her homemade jelly. "They're old friends, they won't care," she would insist, but she left the station wagon idling as we sneaked onto their land at dusk, furtively snipped off vines, and filled the trunk with fragrant bunches. Those adventures were as inexorably tied to the sweetness of her jelly as the wax seals that covered each jar and gave a delightful pop when pressed with the back of a spoon.

When I was about five, I decided to cheer my mother up by picking her a bunch of flowers. That day, my mother had been moping around our cottage in Nauset Heights, looking forlorn. She might have had a fight with her own mother, or maybe she felt frustrated by how long Charles's divorce was taking; I'll never know. Perhaps she was just hung-over from a party the previous night. Whatever the cause, I wanted to make her happier. I always wanted to make my mother happier.

Determined to pick her the most beautiful and bountiful bouquet she'd ever seen, I grabbed the kitchen scissors and embarked upon my mission. I dismissed the daisies that grew weed-like down the grassy center strip of our long dirt driveway, the random tiger lilies that poked through the brush, the dainty tea roses that twined around our picket fence. None were quite right. Then I saw them, the flowers for my mother's bouquet, beckoning me from the top of the hill beyond ours: a zigzagging line of lipstick-colored zinnias in bright oranges, pinks, and purples, winking at me from the garden of our next-door neighbor. Undeniably cheerful flowers. I leveled the patch in three minutes, leaving a trail of decapitated stalks in my wake, never pausing to worry what the neighbors would think.

I floated home, my pinkie looped through the scissors' handle, my arms barely long enough to go around my bounty. At the screen door, I was greeted by my mother with unabashed delight.

"Oh, Rennie," she said, scooping me up along with the flowers and placing me on the counter. "You are the sweetest girl."

My mother must have recognized these were someone's zinnias, but there was no talk of right or wrong, no lecture about private property, no nod toward creating what today is known as a "teachable moment." Instead, my mother arranged the flowers in a vase one stem at a time, first brushing the petals against my nose, then christening each zinnia with a lavish and silly name — Francesca, Philomena, Evangeline — and plunking it in the water. Pleasing my mother came with warm and immediate rewards. A week or so later, when Philomena and her friends started to droop, my mother handed me the scissors and nudged me out the door. I brought home bouquets all summer long.

Then there's our flatware. To this day, among the flotsam that can be found at the bottom of the junk drawer in Malabar's kitchen are errant pieces of Pan Am cutlery, circa the 1970s, tarnished reminders of my early life of crime. After Charles and my mother fell in love, when they were in the thick of their contentious — and, in Charles's case, protracted — divorces, the four of us started to travel by plane with some regularity, flying to Boston, where Charles lived, to Martha's Vineyard, where his family had property, and to various vacation spots.

This was at a time when air travel was luxurious, and we were treated like customers at a fine restaurant; even in coach, hot meals were served with cloth napkins and petite metal silverware. My mother coveted those Pan Am forks and knives. She loathed plastic utensils and liked the idea of having real cutlery for our beach picnics, so whenever we flew, we had a competition of sorts: How many sets could each of us lift? I would press the stewardess call button — thrilling in and of itself — and tell the attendant that my meal had come without utensils, and she would deliver a spare set, along with silver pilot wings. A short while later, I would ring that tantalizing button again and this time announce that I had dropped my fork. The attendant would bring another napkin-wrapped bundle and give me a smile and a wink. My record, I believe, was four sets, scored on a flight to visit my grandparents in Phoenix, Arizona.

I knew only what pleased my mother; I didn't have a moral compass. It would be years before I understood the forces that shaped who she was and who I became and recognized the hurt that we both caused. What I knew then was that nothing made me feel more loved than making my mother happy, and any means justified that end. Starting when I was fourteen, what made my mother happy was Ben Souther. With that, my lying took a dark turn. Lies of omission became lies of commission. What began as choice turned into habit and became my conscience's muscle memory.

In the early summers of their affair, evenings went like this: After Peter and I finished dinner, we rode our bikes to our friends' houses. We had a core group of pals, half of them summer residents, like us, and half of them locals. There were some friends who came and went, but mostly it was a group of about eight of us. We played endless games of spin-the-bottle on the bay beaches below their houses where the air was heavy with salt and the beers in the cooler tinkled like dice. On particularly daring nights, we'd swim out to a floating dock not far from shore, take off our bathing suits underwater, leave them on the raft, and swim, thrilled to be naked yet unseen in one another's presence.

My routine changed once I had my mother's secret and a job to do. When the Southers were visiting, I felt compelled to leave these teen gatherings early so that I could make it home for the tail end of dinner. By the time I arrived, the two couples were usually soused. I would take a few bites of whatever feast my mother had concocted and then innocently suggest we all take a walk—a "constitutional," as my mother called it—knowing Charles and Lily would never join. Who could be suspicious of a postdinner walk with a teenage chaperone? No one. At some point early on, my mother must have told Ben that I was in on their secret, and, apparently, he was unfazed by this fact. After all, my presence made everything possible.

I would take both their hands and tug them toward the door, and out we'd march onto the road singing "I see the moon and the moon sees me." The scene looked like something out of a Norman Rockwell painting, but once the three of us were around the bend and out of the glow of the street lamp, my mother and Ben would kiss passionately, often with me still in the middle, part of a three-way embrace. We were in this love affair together. We'd make our way to the top of the hill, sometimes going a bit beyond but never much. The walks were not the main purpose of our outings. When we circled back, Ben and my mother would veer off the road and slip into the guesthouse, my mother's rental property next door, frequently unoccupied.

I'd wait for them on a rock overlooking the bay at the front of the property and watch the moonlight shimmer on the water's surface. They told me they needed some time to talk and make plans for their next visit. I sat under the lollipop tree, so dubbed by my mother for its charming shape, and listened to the distant thud of waves breaking on the outer beach. From my perch, I imagined that I could hear my mother's dress slipping off, the sound of Ben's kisses across her collarbone, the groan of floorboards beneath their tenderness.

FIVE

M Y LIFE DURING the school year was vastly different than during summers on Cape Cod. For one thing, it was lonely. The mansion Peter and I had called home since our mother married Charles did not encourage familial proximity or interaction. Neither Peter's bedroom nor mine—nor any of the other fifteen bedrooms in the house—was close enough to the family room to allow us to overhear the mumble of our parents' conversations, let alone fall asleep to those distant vibrations. The house was so big that there weren't even distinct smells associated with particular rooms, like cinnamon sugar in the kitchen after our mother perfected her doughnut recipe or the smoke of old fires in the den. Sounds and smells—just about everything, really—disappeared into the vastness.

There was also the fact that 100 Essex had been on the market since the day we arrived, lending a feeling of impermanence to our living situation. The house was impossible to heat in those energy-lean years and even more impossible to sell; the only legitimate offer had come from the Unification Church, aka the Moonies, but accepting a bid that would damage Charles's family's name wasn't an option. What would the neighbors think? So my mother and stepfather did what WASPs have done for generations: they lived off the vapors of family wealth, maintained appearances, and drank copiously.

A day in our life at the time went something like this: Charles shuffled off each morning to work at the investment banking and brokerage firm that his grandfather had founded and that bore his family's name. He disliked this job, but luckily for him, his passion for archaeology offered solace from this stultifying fate. Starting in the tenth grade, my brother attended a different New England prep school than I did. Peter went to Roxbury Latin, an independent, all-boys school, and I went to Milton Academy, an institution with a stately campus featuring sprawling green lawns, well-kept grounds, and imposing red-brick buildings and whose motto was "Dare to be true." And our mother filled her days with . . . well, I was never quite sure with what. She might have been puttering around that enormous residence trying to figure out how to fit in with the country-club set or how to jump-start a new career after having jettisoned the old. Or perhaps she was simply wondering if it had all been a huge mistake.

During the school year, Peter and I ate dinner together at the kitchen table every evening at around six o'clock, right as Malabar and Charles commenced their leisurely cocktail hour. The ritual began with a lively discussion of what they wanted to drink, bourbon or scotch. This was not a decision to be made lightly because it was an evening-long commitment. If they chose bourbon, bourbon it would be, not just for that first drink or two — on the rocks with a splash — but also for their Manhattans, their power pack and its dividend. Very occasionally, rum or rye might make an appearance. But never vodka, or at least never at night (the clear spirit did sometimes find its way into a bloody mary at brunch). And absolutely never gin, which Malabar detested with a passion because her mother, Vivian, had administered it to her starting when she was twelve as a tonic to relieve menstrual cramps. And although Malabar never forgave her mother for eliminating a perfectly good spirit from her cocktail repertoire, she administered the same home remedy to me, creating an association between gin and menstruation that I have not been able to shake to this day.

Once they'd landed on what to drink, Malabar would retrieve the appropriate glassware—tumblers or highballs—and Charles would pour. Then, their moods brightening with anticipation, they'd retreat to the library, where they'd sit on plush sofas, an antique end table dotted with coasters between them. The accumulation of all these cocktail conversations added up to their life together.

—

Starting in 1980, my mother's affair eclipsed nearly everything else in her life. She was radiant and hot with it, blinded for a time. She still did what she could for Charles—hosted dinner parties, accompanied him to events, orchestrated family gatherings—but she could not get enough of Ben Souther.

"Rennie, I've never felt so alive in my life," she confided giddily one day. We were in her bathroom, she sitting on a stool, me standing behind her, my gloved hands applying henna conditioner to her hair. The concoction, just brewed, was the consistency of mud and smelled like wet hay.

"Tell me what it's like," I said, even though we'd had this conversation before and I'd witnessed firsthand how the volatile forces of passion and infidelity had given my mother exuberance. I just loved to hear her talk about it.

"It's like that moment in the *Wizard of Oz* when everything goes from black-and-white to color," she said, twirling her stool to face me, a strand of henna-covered hair slapping across her upper lip and sending beads of conditioner flying, making us both laugh.

"I'm not sure Ben is going to love you with a mustache," I said, returning the stray tress atop its swampy pile and tucking the whole green mess into a clear shower cap. It had left a dark line below my mother's nose, which I wiped clean with a warm washcloth. We did these treatments about once a month, usually on the Sunday before Malabar was to see Ben, when she was at her most jittery.

"Or maybe it's more like diving into a wave," she said. "You brace yourself for what you know is going to happen, but still, it's a shock, right?"

There was so much tightly coiled inside my mother's affair — love, sin, lust — that the situation seemed destined to explode sooner or later. I saw my job as protecting her, and all of us, really, from this eventuality.

I swiveled her around to face the mirror on the back of the door, my head above hers in our reflection. "Mom, what will you do if someone finds out?" I asked.

"No one will ever find out," she assured me. "We're being very careful, Rennie. Plus, we have you, our secret weapon," she added, patting my hands as they rested on her shoulders.

I started the timer. The henna had to stay in for an hour. "But what if someone does?" I persisted. I worried constantly about this. What would happen to her, to us, if the truth came to light?

She leaned in close to the mirror, examining some flaw I couldn't see or perhaps just buying time. "Well, that would be terrible, and I don't even like to think about it, as it would kill Charles and Lily too," she said. "They're both fragile enough as it is. But if it were to happen, Ben and I would stay together. We've made that promise to each other."

In the beginning, Malabar had been as nervous as I was about getting caught, so we were meticulous in covering her tracks. We developed complex alibis for her trysts in New York; she was either visiting her best friend, Brenda, who was single and had a busy career, or, more often, attending to her ailing stepmother, Julia, my grandfather's much younger second wife. Julia, just a couple of years older than my mother, was a binge drinker with a long history of alcoholic episodes; "benders," our family called them. It was a perfect ruse. My grandfather had died a year earlier, so my mother's cover would not require his corroboration. Also, she had intervened to help Julia in the past, so the lie felt close enough to the truth that it passed effortlessly from our lips.

When I felt bad that we were hiding my mother's secret by exposing my step-grandmother's, Malabar assured me that Julia's alcoholism was not remotely under wraps.

"When you're a falling-down drunk, it's not a well-kept secret, even if you live on Fifth Avenue. Trust me, Rennie, despite what Julia wishes to believe, everyone knows she has a serious problem."

This was likely true. Julia did fantastically outlandish things when drunk, from stripping down to her underwear at dinner parties to passing out in a hallway where unsuspecting guests might stumble upon her in a pool of urine. With stories like Julia's at my disposal, it would be easy to throw people off Malabar's scent if it came to that.

When the timer went off, Malabar showered and washed the henna out of her hair and we moved from the master bathroom to her dressing room, possibly the only room in 100 Essex that could be described as cozy. It was our favorite place to talk. Furnished with a twin bed, a floral-skirted dressing table, a matching upholstered stool, and complementary drapes, the room was heavy with fabric and felt feminine in an old-fashioned way. My mother, who'd suffered from insomnia since Christopher's death, usually slept in this room, ostensibly because Charles snored. When I roused her in the mornings, never easy, her head was sandwiched between two pillows with only her nose peeking out.

I took my usual perch on her bed, my back against the wall and my feet tucked under me to make room for her suitcase, which lay open at the foot. We were deciding what she should bring for an overnight stay in New York with Ben. My mother tried on outfit after outfit, appraising her reflection in the full-length mirror, her lips pursed critically.

When she put on a dark green wrap dress that flattered her narrow waist, I said, "Oh, Mom. That's the one. You look gorgeous." And she did.

Malabar positioned herself on the padded stool and leaned into an unforgiving, three-paneled magnified mirror to study her face. Her large brown eyes, shaded by heavy lids, gave her a sultry look. As a child, I'd heard her friend Brenda refer to them as "bedroom eyes." At the time, I took this to mean she looked sleepy.

Despite my assurances that she was beautiful, so very beautiful, Malabar was in no mood for compliments. She pinched the excess skin from her upper lid and frowned at her reflection. "There is nothing worse for a woman than getting old, Rennie," she told me. "My mother warned me and I didn't believe her. But mark my words: *Nothing worse on earth.*"

A photograph of my glamorous grandmother Vivian sat on the dressing table. Hers was the beauty standard against which my mother compared herself and believed she came up short. I didn't agree. To me, Malabar was far lovelier. My mother's face had warmth, and her eyes sparkled with mischief, whereas my grandmother's black hair, dark eyes, and flawless ivory skin struck me as austere. She had a steely gaze even when she smiled. When I looked at my grandmother's photo, it occurred to me how all-consuming it must have been for my mother to be her only child.

But I was alone in the impression that my mother was the more attractive of the two. I needed only to utter my grandmother's name, and the universal response — from men, women, close friends, and rivals — was that Vivian was the most stunning woman who had ever walked the earth.

"Your grandmother was a seductress extraordinaire for much of her life, but she did not age gracefully," my mother said. I'd heard stories about my grandmother's temper, competitiveness, and alcoholism for years, including one about a terrible fight she'd had with my mother when I was a toddler. They'd brawled over a man they'd both been flirting with at a party. Drunk and furious, they slung accusations until the argument turned physical and my mother ended up falling backwards and landing in the fireplace. My grandmother came out of it bruised, my mother in a hip-to-toe cast.

I hated to imagine them fighting; the thought of a mother hurting her daughter scared me.

My grandmother was bedridden now, no longer capable of tussling with her only child or seducing a man. After she and my grandfather divorced for the second time, she spent some thirty years single and then remarried in 1976. Her new husband, Gregory, hailed from Plymouth and was a direct descendant of the Pilgrims, just like Ben Souther. But happiness and misfortune ran hand in hand for Vivian, and Gregory died just five months after their wedding, when I was eleven. My grandmother, wanting to be clearheaded at his funeral, skipped her blood-thinning medication and had a major stroke the next day. We visited her regularly, but she was no longer capable of communicating in a meaningful way. Years later, my mother confessed that my grandmother had had a decade-long affair with Gregory while she waited for his wife to die. It was as if Vivian had left a map for her daughter to follow.

Initially, my mother and Ben conducted their romance cautiously, meeting discreetly on Ben's business trips, usually in New York City, where he served on the board of several organizations. They would book hotel rooms on different floors from each other, order room service instead of going out for meals, and pay for everything with cash. But it wasn't long before they became emboldened, having determined that it was unlikely they'd run into anyone they knew. They started dining out in style at restaurants like Le Cirque, Hatsuhana, Lutèce, and La Tulipe, which was owned by one of my mother's good friends.

My mother loved nothing more than going to fine restaurants, insisting it was the only way for her to get out of her own kitchen. "Think about it, Rennie," she told me more than once. "When you are known to be a fabulous cook, everyone's too intimidated to invite you over for dinner."

This might have sounded arrogant, but it was true. My mother had studied at Le Cordon Bleu in Paris, had worked as a chef in Time-Life's test kitchens for its Food of the World series, had published four cookbooks, and currently wrote a popular food column, Do-Ahead Dining, for the *Boston Globe*. What rational person would risk judgment by inviting Malabar over for a tuna casserole?

Restaurants were like mini-vacations for Malabar; someone else was doing her job. She adored getting dressed up, curling her shiny, auburn hair, and applying a slash of bright lipstick, keenly aware that when she entered a room, people took notice. She was daring when it came to ordering food and rarely went for old favorites like lamb chops or filet mignon, opting instead to see just what the chefs had in them, exactly what they could do with something challenging like sweetbreads or razor clams. She had the uncanny ability to know how a dish was prepared from a single bite—whether, say, the meat had been seared or poached first—and could tick off every ingredient in a sauce, store that information, and not only replicate it later but make it a bit better. "When it comes to cooking, I'm a thief," she'd whisper to me, her exhale fragrant with spices.

Soon, she and Ben started traveling together on the same flights to New York City, even booking seats beside each other. Once, she reported they'd run into someone they knew on the Boston-to-New York shuttle, an acquaintance from Plymouth who knew both Charles and Ben. My heart raced. *What if that got back to Charles?* But my mother said that she simply placed one hand on Ben's sleeve, another on her breastbone, and exclaimed with surprise: "What a small world. First I bump into Ben Souther, and now you!" Then she'd invited the person to join them.

I hung on every word of my mother's stories, eager for details of her clandestine and illicit encounters with Ben, which occurred every four to six weeks. Sometimes I would leave a note on her pillow instructing her to wake me up as soon as she returned from New York. She would, and we'd talk on my bed into the middle of the night about how in love with Ben she was. There were never any reports of Broadway shows, trips to the Metropolitan Museum of Art, strolls along Park Avenue; there was no evidence of shopping binges. As far as I could tell, my mother and Ben spent their time together engaged exclusively in life's most sacred sensual duet: eating and making love. Luckily for me, my mother preferred to talk about the food and not the sex, although every so often her coy smile revealed less chaste memories.

Whole Sundays could be lost in my mother's dressing room, me on her soft bed, propped up by pillows, Malabar sitting on her dressing-table stool. I never tired of hearing her talk about Ben or of dissecting his every sweet promise. My mother loved nothing more than imagining the future they would one day have together, especially when it came to travel.

"Let's talk honeymoon, Rennie," she'd say and we would review the top contenders: a lavish Italian extravaganza, an African safari, a sailing adventure along the Turkish coastline. I was always drawn to the idea of the safari—all those magnificent animals—but my mother, more attuned to thread count and truffle oil, wanted the decadence of Italy. "Is there a more romantic spot on earth?" she asked.

Much to my mother's frustration, Ben was reluctant to participate in these fantasies. He had established strict rules for this affair, best policies to navigate its moral ambiguities and avoid getting caught. These included planning only one visit ahead, not calling my mother from his home unless it was for official couple-friendship business, and never committing his feelings to paper.

Ben seemed to have it all: a satisfying domestic situation with Lily, of whom he was very fond, a fabulous romantic life with Malabar, with whom he was in love, and the ability to compartmentalize the two, which exasperated my mother no end. My mother wanted their affair to be as all-consuming for him as it was for her. She had to settle for it being as all-consuming for me. I lapped up every detail, utterly engrossed.

"You know what I'd like to do with Ben's rules?" she'd ask me. I knew the answer but was never given the chance to respond. "Break every single one of them."

The power of transgression, seductive in and of itself.

"I just have to be patient, Rennie," my mother would say over and over again, as much to herself as to me, both of us knowing patience was not her strong suit. "I need to play the long game here."

And where was Charles when we had these Sunday talks? Usually in an armchair tucked into a corner of the den, a standing lamp behind him illuminating whatever large book was on his lap, his index finger tracking his place on the page. My stepfather, a reserved man whose destiny — set by his father and grandfather — was the unromantic work of making money, was also an unlikely dreamer, a man inspired by early American history and stories of ships lost at sea.

It's worth pointing out that there was a time when my mother was as crazy about Charles as she now was about Ben. She'd been charmed by Charles's intellect, in particular his longtime interest in the Pilgrims and the culture they'd created in Plymouth. And though she loved that Charles came from family money, she admired that he was driven by passion and not the desire to acquire more wealth. He would read and ponder until right around six o'clock, at which point his internal alarm clock would go off and he would emerge from his peaceful sanctuary, suddenly animated, and promise my mother a cocktail if she would only listen to his latest obsession. Before Ben, my mother would happily comply.

But falling in love with Ben had upended Malabar's priorities. She was no longer as aroused as she had once been by Charles's brilliant mind, his archaeological and historical obsessions, his genteel manners. She still took her evening libation with her husband, but I'm quite sure she daydreamed of Ben as Charles spoke, now craving stimulation of a different sort. Ben was outgoing, physical, confident to a fault. She wanted him.

Whenever my mother was away—purportedly rescuing Julia but in reality staying in a hotel room with her husband's best friend—it was my job to look after Charles. This task was not difficult. The most I had to do was reheat a meal my mother had prepared in advance, open a bottle of wine, or help him undo the buttons on his shirtsleeves, as the fine-motor skills involved in that process were no longer possible for him. Really, the man just wanted peace, a stiff cocktail, and a quiet place to read and think. What made Charles a great stepfather was probably what had made him a less-than-stellar father to his own children—his parenting style was one of benign neglect. He was uninterested in parenting Peter and me, in the messy feuds, the inherent competition, the demands on his time and energy.

The only hard part about taking care of Charles was the lying.

I had to confirm Malabar's alibi, corroborating her story if only with my silence. At first, it felt simple. But over time that silence became a heavy weight. When you lie to someone you love—and I did love Charles—let alone when you lie so often that the lie seems truer than the actual truth, you lose the only thing that matters: the possibility of real connection. I lost the ability to connect with Charles the day the first lie fell from my lips.

Over time, I began to lose it with myself too.

By the second half of tenth grade, I had stomachaches all the time. My mother took me to a specialist, who suggested the pain might be stress-related. Without my mother in the room, the doctor asked me about my extracurricular activities, my social life. Did I have lots of friends at school? I assured her that I did, but the truth was I had not knit myself into the fabric of the Milton community. I had more acquaintances than close friends, did not play team sports or involve myself much in afterschool clubs. Did I have a boyfriend?

she wanted to know. "A pretty girl like you must have a lot of suitors," she said.

I did not, but I knew better than to explain that the bulk of my romantic energy was spent in the service of my mother.

"Oh, you know, I have some crushes," I said truthfully, and this seemed to satisfy her. "But most of the boys in my grade are immature. Plus I need to focus on my schoolwork."

"What kind of grades do you get?" she asked.

"Pretty much straight As," I said.

She nodded knowingly. "That's likely the problem. You're a perfectionist. I think perhaps you need to relax your standards. Go easier on yourself."

When my mother joined us in the examining room, the doctor suggested the demands of Milton's academic environment might be the source of my stress and that I could be developing an ulcer. She suggested that I avoid sodas, caffeine, and spicy and acidic foods.

"Thank you so much," my mother said to the doctor with a sigh of relief. "I'm sure this is all my fault. As Rennie probably told you, I can be a bit exuberant with the cayenne." She laughed and looked at me. "And you, young lady, have to concern yourself less with the As and get out more. Honestly, life's too short!"

On our drive home, I thought about my latest reading assignment, *The Scarlet Letter* by Nathaniel Hawthorne. I wondered if my mother felt any of Hester Prynne's shame, if Ben was beset by Arthur Dimmesdale's guilty conscience, or if they would have dismissed the novel as puritanical schlock, as my father had.

My mother insisted that she felt not one whit of guilt about the affair. "Here's how you need to think about it, Rennie," she told me. "Ben and I didn't mean to fall in love. It just happened. The important thing is that we have chosen to put Charles and Lily first. Neither of us wants to hurt them. You understand that, right?"

I nodded.

"Leaving them would wreck their lives. Divorce is messy and

painful, and it's nothing anyone wants. Plus, Charles and Lily are not in good health. This news would make their situations worse. So, really, Ben and I are acting altruistically here. As are you, sweetie." She patted my thigh. "You are helping us to do the right thing. The plan is to honor our wedding vows—until death us do part. Does that make sense?"

It did and, oh, how I loved it when my mother spoke to me this way, woman to woman, absolutely nothing but trust and honesty between us. At last, I understood the immensity of my mother and Ben's sacrifice. The plan was to wait for Lily and Charles to die. It was the narrative they'd settled on. At the time, it struck me as noble and even kind.

SIX

WITH CHARLES AND BEN'S long friendship as cover, my mother courted a relationship with Ben's wife. Lily was famous for her English-style flower gardens, abundant and robust, that stretched along both sides of their large lawn and wrapped around their house. She did all the work herself, spent hours bent over digging, planting, fertilizing, and weeding, and her gardens were immaculate. My mother cooed over them, showered Lily with compliments. To me, she confessed that she didn't understand the fuss. "Tidy rows. Sturdy stems. Color, of course. But, really, where's the creativity?"

What my mother chose to see in Lily's industriousness was a lack of imagination and a rigidity, an attempt to wield control and impose order, and she assumed that this was how Lily conducted herself in her marriage as well. "Ben is like a wild animal," my mother said in a way that made me understand that we'd left the topic of gardening. "The man needs a jungle." My thoughts went to the untamed tangle of rose hips that scrambled along the banks of our property and the shorebirds that feasted in the sand flats below. I imagined Ben would be happy here.

My mother also developed an interest in Ben and Lily's two children, Jack and Hannah, who were in their early twenties when the affair began. I had yet to meet either of the Souther kids but I became intrigued by them too. Jack was a California lifeguard in the summer and a Colorado ski patroller in the winter; Hannah was an equestrienne in Massachusetts. My mother speculated that these professions might be disappointing to their MIT graduate and businessman father. Lily had kept a series of leather-bound diaries of her children's early years, with lengthy entries describing their dispositions, activities, and which foods did and did not appeal. And although Malabar pored over these pages with Lily admiringly, she scoffed at them to me privately. "So much time spent on pureed peas!"

That said, in her own children's baby albums — Christopher's, Peter's, and mine — Malabar did much the same. She wrote hilariously about our likes and dislikes, taped tufts of our white-blond hair to the black pages, and drew diagrams of our open mouths with arrows and dates to indicate which teeth came in when. In entertaining captions, she listed our talents and aversions, attempting to capture each of our baby essences at age one. Christopher: *Crawls forward* and *backward, shreds newspaper, grabs everything!* Peter: *Bad temper and willfulness!* Rennie: *No talents, but appetite!*

And there were the Southers' trips. All those trips, dozens of expeditions to far-flung places, from China and India to the Galápagos, to Mexico and Argentina, all over Europe — Scotland, Denmark, France, and Spain — to Africa and every part of America. Ben had run a company in Boston that had subsidiaries in thirty different countries, so many of these trips had been work-related, but just as many had been for pleasure. Aghast, my mother told me of week- and even month-long gaps in Jack's and Hannah's baby journals when Lily was off gallivanting somewhere with Ben. "What kind of mother could leave her children for so long?" Malabar wondered aloud. "It's monstrous."

I was appalled right along with Malabar, adopting her feelings as my own, but I could tell that the Southers' trips were a genuine source of envy. Although Ben was retired, he was still active on many boards and organized his life around fishing and hunting adventures. My mother coveted a life of travel like the one her father had had with her stepmother, Julia. Between Julia's stays at the Betty Ford Center, my grandparents were always in some fabulous hotel in some exotic country. Charles had given my mother a comfortable life, but his globetrotting days were far behind him.

The long and short of it was that even Lily found Malabar beguiling. Who could blame her? When my mother aimed her light at you, let it shine on you and allowed you to feel that you held her interest and amused her, it was nearly impossible to look away. Malabar could be intensely charismatic, a breath of fresh air, an irresistible combination of clever and irreverent, and Lily was enchanted. Soon enough, the two couples were spending even more time together and the Southers became our most frequent summer houseguests on Cape Cod. They visited regularly, allowing my mother and Ben's romance to carry on apace, nearly in plain view.

Still, it was never enough. My mother was ravenous for more time with Ben. She felt despair during the weeks and sometimes months between their encounters.

"Rennie, I don't think I can stand this anymore," she said once, frantic after Ben and Lily had postponed an upcoming weekend visit.

"What happened?" I asked.

"Some damn flower thing of Lily's. There's a group touring gardens in Plymouth and Lily's is part of the circuit."

We were on Cape Cod for a late-September weekend, a bittersweet time full of reminders of previous pleasures — our hammock down, the boats pulled, the marsh grass becoming golden brown. My mother and Ben had just celebrated their one-year anniversary. I was about to turn sixteen.

"Think, Rennie. We need to think. How do we get the Southers to the Cape more often?" my mother asked. "The more time Ben spends with me, the more time he'll need to spend with me."

We were in the kitchen, as usual, my mother testing a recipe for the next week's Do-Ahead Dining column, a savory autumn stew. She tossed a handful of smoked sausage into a pot of French lentils, stirred angrily.

"Bite?" she asked, blowing on a spoonful.

I nodded and opened my mouth. I'd been taste-testing for my mother for as long as I could remember. I rolled the mouthful over my tongue — toasted cumin seeds, still-firm lentils, a rich tomato base, some spice. The kielbasa was deliciously salty but hadn't yet mingled adequately with the rest of the mélange.

"Good, not great," I said. "Needs something." I didn't remind my mother that this was the type of spicy, acidic dish that bothered my stomach.

"What a food snob you've become," Malabar said with pride. "I suppose you'd prefer Tibetan yak in your stew? Or perhaps the perfectly marbled earlobes of a Wagyu cow, massaged just to your liking?"

Suddenly my mother's expression changed as the shards of an idea raced toward her like iron filings to a magnet.

"Oh. My. God. Rennie. That's it." Malabar leaned across the counter, took my face in her hands, and kissed my forehead. "Rennie, you are the most brilliant child in the world."

I lived for moments like this with Malabar. Even though I didn't understand exactly what I'd said or done to solve my mother's problem, it was enough to know that I had helped. As I listened to my mother tell me her grand idea, my heart raced with excitement. Together, we'd come up with just about the most ingenious plan ever concocted.

A few weeks later, we were able to launch our rocket of an idea. My mother had looped Ben in on the details during one of their exceedingly rare phone calls, and they both agreed that my participation was key.

It was early October by then, the harbor empty of all boats other than those belonging to the most intrepid commercial lobstermen, and even those would be pulled in the coming days. Ben had just returned from his annual black-tailed deer hunt at a ranch in San Felipe, California, and he and Lily arrived bearing venison steaks and a pound of lustrous liver, which my mother immediately skinned, sliced, and placed into a dish of buttermilk to extract the blood. Charles, seated on his usual tall stool, the one closest to the bar with its shakers and stirrers, perked up at the sight of his dear friends. Immediately, Ben started telling us the story of how he'd fallen out of a pickup truck, unnoticed by his buddies, after consuming a fifth of bourbon.

"On that note, Ben, why don't you make everyone a cocktail?" my mother suggested.

Charles yielded his host duties without a word, and Ben made a round of drinks while my mother got busy with the liver. She pinched oregano and sage leaves from her herb garden and sautéed them in butter and garlic, infusing the kitchen with their heady fragrance. Next, she caramelized shallots and other vegetables and, in a separate pan, sautéed the shiny slabs of liver.

Malabar was still in the kitchen when the rest of us put on jackets, went out into the crisp autumn air, and sat in a semicircle around the deck table, its center umbrella lowered and strapped for the season. The sun was making its descent behind us, casting long shafts of light across the harbor and creating the illusion that the marsh grass was on fire, glowing golden from beneath the surface of the water. From inside, the *whir* of the Cuisinart sounded as my mother blended the liver and vegetables, no doubt adding chunks of soft butter and salt flakes. Across the windswept bay, we heard terns screeching, and suddenly dozens materialized before us and dived toward some underwater disturbance. Then the surface of the water broke with a thrash of fins — what my father called "a bluefish blitz" — and thousands of minnows leaped to escape the fish hunting them below, only to be snatched up in the beaks of black-capped terns above.

I studied Ben as he observed the carnage. His body twitched the way some men's bodies do when they watch a football game, imagining that they are catching the pass. I could tell he would have liked to grab a rod and dash down to the water—which was what my father or Peter would have done—but instead, hearing the rapping on the glass slider, he turned to help my mother, who stood on the other side holding a large round serving board. They beamed at each other as she slipped past.

The birds dispersed and their feeding frenzy ended as ours began.

Malabar lowered the artfully arranged predinner offerings: paper-thin slices of ruby-red venison carpaccio under dollops of horseradish crème fraîche, a bowl of wrinkled and briny olives, two triangles of overly ripe cheese oozing past their soft rinds, and a dish of her ethereally smooth venison pâté tucked in beside a collection of cornichons and slices of pickled onion. The tray was a thing of beauty, each delicacy separated by sprigs of rosemary from my mother's herb garden and garnished with Lily's nasturtium flowers.

Malabar admired her handiwork and let loose a hearty laugh. "If something on this board doesn't kill us, I'm not sure what will," she said, raising her glass. "To salmonella!"

"Legionnaires'," Charles toasted.

I raised my glass and took a big swig of ginger ale.

"Bring on the bacteria!" Ben said, taking hold of Malabar's free hand. My mother had long, slender fingers that curved up like ski tips at the ends. She kept her nails filed into sharp points, ten tiny daggers. Ben kissed her palm. "Malabar, I can think of no better way to go than to be poisoned by you."

The ice-cold soda got stuck on a knot of remorse in the back of my throat.

Lily registered my distress by rolling her eyes at me, a look that I took to mean *I'm not worried, so don't you be. Pay no attention to these old fools.* Seeing Lily's lack of concern, I relaxed a bit. Still, something on my face had given away my concern, and I felt sick that

Lily had seen it. *Stupid*, I chided myself, and I willed Ben and Malabar to be less obvious.

My mother spread generous scoopfuls of venison pâté over thin slices of toasted and buttered French bread and placed one round onto each of our open palms as if bestowing the Host at Communion. We popped them whole into our mouths; the flavors and textures settled over our tongues as the whipped and gamy layers revealed themselves in slow motion.

"Heavenly," Ben said, his words muffled around his mouthful. Charles nodded.

"Wait! Everyone, I have an idea," my mother announced dramatically, bringing her hands down on the table.

I perked up. This was my cue. My mother and I had practiced how to mortar each brick into this storyline, and it was critical to get Charles and Lily onboard. This conversation could not be solely my mother and Ben. That wouldn't look good. My role was crucial.

Malabar took a leisurely, palate-cleansing sip of her power pack. Her audience leaned in. "What do you think about" — she paused for effect — "a wild-game cookbook?"

I took another sip of ginger ale and waited a beat.

Charles's eyebrows lifted in contemplation; he was no doubt imagining what the next year of test dinners might promise. He'd been enjoying the fruits of Malabar's labor with her Do-Ahead Dining column, but this had not always been the case. Early in their marriage, my mother had agreed to put together a charity cookbook for the middle school that Peter and I attended. The other parents, decidedly unsophisticated cooks, submitted recipes, and for one very long year, Malabar tested the gelatinous, one-dish casseroles. Charles would arrive home in the evening, take a look at my mother hunched over the stove, the telltale red notebook on its stand, and cringe. "Sweet, no. Not another test night."

"What exactly counts as wild game?" I asked now. "Sounds a bit gross — just meat, meat, and more meat?"

"Oh, Rennie, not at all," my mother said. "Our cookbook can be whatever we want it to be. It should definitely include seafood; just look at the bounty out there. And vegetables, the types you can forage for. Lily, you could teach me about mushrooming."

Lily smiled at the thought of having a role.

"But *who* would buy it?" I said, playing devil's advocate, my tone hinting that the adults were out of touch. "Not everyone has a hunter in their midst. You guys are the exception, not the rule. All this" — I pointed to the tray of appetizers — "is not exactly normal."

"Normal, my dear," my mother said in her most regal voice, "is not something I've ever aspired to be."

"Okay, fine. You're not normal, Mom. But not one kid at my school eats pheasant or rabbit. There will be, like, ten people who'll buy this book."

"I disagree, Rennie," Lily said.

I exhaled; she had taken the bait.

"Think of all the people who are becoming dismayed by the food industry these days, with how we raise meat in this country," she continued. "The chemicals. The pesticides. The conditions."

Hook, line, sinker.

My mother blinked love my way, Morse code–style, and Ben tapped his knee against mine under the table.

"Brilliant idea, sweet," Charles said to my mother, and he reminded us that his children all loved to fish and hunt. "Count me in."

"Me too, Malabar," said Lily. "What fun it will be."

Ben placed his hands behind his head and tipped back in his chair. "Hold everything," he said, his smile enormous. "Not so fast. We haven't discussed royalties. Seems to me that the hunter-gatherer couple should get a greater cut than the cooking-eating couple."

"Oh, Ben." Lily laughed. "You stop that this minute."

"Do we have a title?" asked Charles.

Ben and my mother were silent for a moment. They looked upward, as if a title might fall from the sky.

"How about something simple?" Malabar said. "We could call it *Wild Game*. It tells the reader what to expect but promises adventure too."

"It's perfect," Lily said.

Ben touched his glass to my mother's. "To our wild game, Malabar."

SEVEN

OUR HOME on Cape Cod became the hub of the wild-game universe. Wood ducks hung in the shed to dry-age; rabbits were butch-
ered and sautéed; mussels, clams, and lobsters, separated by layers
of seaweed, were slow-cooked over coals in giant pits down on the
beach. Holes were dug, fires built, and hunks of meat were swabbed
with olive oil, rosemary, and crushed garlic. The hypnotic hiss of
fat dripping onto coals was the backdrop to almost every meal. Malabar, expert at extracting all things comestible from any creature,
kept her enormous enameled Dutch oven, blackened at the base, in
constant use on the back burner of the stove, braising tough cuts
of meat, rendering shiny chunks of fat, simmering marrow-filled
bones.

Whenever Ben burst through our door with diminutive Lily in
tow, he would always bring something unexpected — green frogs
from his pond or a squirrel that he'd hit in his rush to get to us —
in addition to the agreed-upon fare that was to be the next night's
dinner. My mother would cook a light meal when they arrived, and
we would discuss the following night's feast, brainstorming about
how best to prepare it. Often, I'd never tried the meat — bison or

alligator or wigeon—but Ben would describe it and I was encouraged to toss out ideas. *What if we slid butter and tarragon leaves under the skin? How about slow-roasting it until the meat falls off the bones? Something sweet in the sauce, like figs or currants?*

Ben was the most experienced game eater among us, boasting that he'd tried everything he'd ever killed, from a two-ounce black rail to a six-ton elephant. He even ate notoriously bad-tasting animals, like the fishy sea ducks locally known as skunk-heads, insisting they were palatable if you removed the rank fat and then flash-fried them. He suggested my mother develop a recipe.

"*Wild Game* is not intended to be a survivalist manifesto, Ben. It will be a *gourmet* cookbook," my mother said. She looked Lily's way and shook her head, feigning annoyance.

"Malabar, you don't even know the half of it," Lily said, basking in her friend's sympathy.

Looking back, I can't imagine that Charles and Lily did not see what was going on before their eyes. Could they not smell and taste foreboding each time they sat down to one of my mother's meals, Frank Sinatra's *Songs for Swingin' Lovers!* piped into the dining room and arching over their heads? Their spouses' fingers touched at every passed plate. Their eyes lingered. Malabar's laughter dared the room to imagine her thoughts.

Together, my mother and Ben shucked oysters, plucked feathers from mallards, ripped innards out of delicate woodland creatures. Their patter was filled with pornographic double-entendres about the game they roasted, the savory *loins,* luscious *breasts,* tender *thighs.* Their every gesture seemed garishly sensual; the way they slurped clams from their shells, gnawed on bones and sucked out the marrow, and dipped their pinkies into the leftover sauce on their plates. Never mind that when they moaned their delight, the sound caused my stomach to pinch and sent me upstairs for Tums, which I ingested by the handful.

Through it all, Charles and Lily went along for the ride, chewing and tasting, earnestly selecting one piece of elk, brook trout, or grouse over another for the sound reason of moistness or flavor. They took their jobs as testers seriously. Lily even jotted down her impressions in a small spiral notebook. Charles looked pleased when their tastes aligned. They had an unspoken alliance of sorts as the voices of reason, the grownups, when Ben and my mother's mock arguments got out of hand or when their ideas became too outlandish.

"Malabar," Ben said, eyes twinkling. "How does a woman attend Le Cordone Blue and not know a goddamn thing about butchering meat?"

Lily rushed to Malabar's defense. "Oh, please, Ben. Don't be a fool. Anyone can butcher meat. Butchers are a dime a dozen."

"It's 'Le Cordon Bleu,'" my mother said, correcting Ben's pronunciation. For months, she'd tried to teach him to enunciate the final *s* in *vichyssoise* so he sounded more sophisticated. She pointed the tip of a sharp filleting knife in Ben's direction. "Your game would be as tough as shoe leather were it not for me."

"Give it up now, Ben," Charles warned his friend. "You will never, ever win with Malabar." He gazed at my mother admiringly. "But there is no sweeter defeat. How about another glass of wine?"

The clues were everywhere, strewn like seaweed on the shore. Did Ben accidentally just call my mother "darling"? Did anyone hear my mother suggest they re-create that sauce they'd had at Lutèce?

And what of all their sudden disappearances?

"Ben, be a dear," my mother would say, dredging a slab of shad roe through lightly seasoned flour, "fetch the charcoal. It's in the far corner of the basement, near the garden tools."

"Malabar." Ben's voice would creep up through the floorboards a few minutes later. "Can you give me a hand? I don't see it."

My mother would wipe her palms on her apron or a nearby dishtowel and give Lily an artful look of good-humored exasperation and camaraderie, a look that said, *Men*. Then she'd pop off to the basement to help Ben.

These moments terrified me more than almost any other. Time slowed down; my stomach burned and my pulse rang in my ears as if I were the one about to get caught. I knew my role at these times. I was there to distract and amuse; I'd talk too much, tell jokes, do a jig in the kitchen if that's what it took conceal Ben and my mother's absence. As if any amount of jazz hands and blathering could divert attention from the ticktock of the grandfather clock and how absurdly long it was taking two adults to locate a ten-pound bag of charcoal.

Footsteps would finally thump back up, five or six or seven minutes later. An eternity.

"Exactly where I told him it would be," my mother would announce.

I'd vigilantly check her for mussed hair, smeared lipstick, disheveled clothing, but if I brushed a strand of hair back into place or straightened her collar, my mother was just as likely to slap my hand in annoyance as to be grateful. She did not sheepishly avoid eye contact or busy herself in the kitchen at these times. If anything, there was defiance in her eyes, a raised chin. She felt the right to what small piece of Ben she had, to what dim glow of the bright light of her future she could bask in now — and, goddamn it, no one was going to take that from her.

Could it be that Lily, then married to Ben for close to forty years, believed her husband to be a harmless flirt and didn't let it bother her? I imagine it would have been inconceivable to Charles that Ben, his oldest friend and godfather to his son, could be in love with his wife, let alone be having an affair with her. I would later learn that before my mother and Charles married, Ben Souther had been one of several people who were suspicious of her intentions. He'd cautioned Charles, one of Boston's most eligible bachelors at the time, not to rush into marriage with her.

So even as evidence stacked up and my mother and Ben's chemistry charged the air, Charles and Lily didn't waver in their support of this friendship or of the wild-game cookbook in the making. Perhaps somewhere deep down, they understood, as I did—for my mother was very clear on this point—that this affair was being conducted with everyone's best interest at heart.

But Malabar was growing impatient. How was she to manage unfulfillment lurking on one side and Charles's death calling from the other? Simple. She filled a shaker with ice, poured in the bourbon, and wrapped herself in a blanket of alcohol to dull the hurt and deaden the guilt as she rode around and around, endlessly circling the life she wanted, that gold ring just out of reach. When Malabar made a power pack, that dry Manhattan with a twist, she would pause for a moment, consider the shaker, then add another shot of booze.

For years when I made Manhattans, I did the same.

EIGHT

AT AGE SEVENTEEN, three years into my life as Malabar's confidante and accomplice, I became overwhelmed by the desire to get away. The gnawing guilt I felt but didn't recognize as such continued to worsen, as did my stomach problems. At the time, I didn't trace the roots of my wanderlust to my mother or anything beyond a typical teenage drive for independence. As my high-school graduation loomed in the spring of 1983, I impulsively decided to take a gap year before attending college. I'd worked hard at Milton Academy and deserved a break, I told myself. I'd earned a year off to follow my dreams. Who could fault me for wanting to travel?

With an acceptance letter from Columbia safely tucked in my desk drawer, I deferred for a year, wondering if my parents might object. Perhaps they'd suggest that I should spend the time doing something meaningful, like volunteering for Habitat for Humanity or teaching English abroad, something that might count as vaguely productive, educational, or altruistic. But I needn't have worried. My family wasn't particularly big on the idea of giving back or community service. I was taught to take full credit for my accomplishments and consider them the result of grit and hard work. *Privilege* was not a concept we discussed in relation to our good fortune.

So, while Malabar expressed concern over how she would possibly manage without me, she did not bat an eye over my ill-conceived plan to explore America starting on the island of Maui. Years ago, we'd spent several family vacations there with my grandfather and Julia. Julia had inherited his beautiful time-share condominium in Napili Kai, and she offered me the use of it starting in mid-June. After that, who knew? I planned to take things one day at a time.

"You just can't miss a single one of our therapy sessions," my mother said, a reference to our private joke that I was the best psychiatrist she'd ever had, not to mention the cheapest. "Promise you'll call every week. We're two halves of the same whole, Rennie. I can't bear to be apart from you for long."

With some sixth sense about my need to get away from Malabar, my father gave me an open-ended round-trip airline ticket to Hawaii as a graduation gift. Although he and I never spoke directly about my relationship with Malabar, he intuited that my mother lacked boundaries with me, as her mother had with her.

I said goodbye to my family and goodbye to 100 Essex, the home I'd lived in from the time I was eight. My mother and Charles had finally found a respectable buyer for the house and would move to an apartment they'd bought on Beacon Hill. Peter was attending Trinity College in Hartford, Connecticut. When I got back, nothing would be the same.

My plan was upended from the start. Unbeknownst to anyone, Julia had gone on another bender that spring and forgotten to reserve her unit in time for my arrival, so I landed on the island, seventeen years old, with a denim duffle bag and no place to stay. I decided that being adrift was an essential part of my adventure, so I spent the first few nights sleeping on the beach under the star-sprayed blackness, feeling powerfully independent for the first time in my life.

Soon enough, things fell into place. I found a studio apartment in

Napili Village and work at a gimmicky jewelry store called the Pearl Factory in Kaanapali, a five-mile shot down Honoapiilani Highway. At the store, shoppers would choose a pre-seeded oyster from a large tank. I would hold up the selected mollusk theatrically as a small crowd gathered and ask if they were absolutely positive that this was the one they wanted. Then, as a hush fell over my audience, I would slip in the knife, pry open the shell, and, with great fanfare, pluck out its iridescent occupant with a pair of silver tongs and greet it with a hearty *Aloha!*

A handsome blond *haole*, as we non-natives were called, started visiting my shop. From Kansas originally, Adam was unlike any of the boys I knew from Boston. He rarely had a plan that stretched beyond the current day. He hung out along the white beaches of Kaanapali and cruised the paved walking path that meandered between the shops and hotels, selling dime bags of weed to tourists. But each evening when the conch shell was blown, a resonant blast announcing that the sun was about to set—one part local tradition, two parts vacationer-cocktail-gong—Adam would materialize in front of the Pearl Factory holding a piña colada–filled coconut. Then off we'd go, aimlessly strolling the beach and talking about our lives.

As our romance proceeded over weeks and months, our walks extended beyond the sandy edges of hotel shorelines to secluded spots tucked into the corrugated volcanic coastline. There, in the nooks and crannies of Maui, in its dark and secret caves, something feather-light unfurled inside me as new physical sensations obliterated all I'd ever known. I was falling in love for the first time. The promise of wonders to come.

Adam showed me Maui's bountiful arcade of outdoor pleasures —hidden waterfalls, rock stacks left by *menehune*, blowholes blasting of water and vapor up through submerged lava tubes. He also introduced me to pot—*pakalolo*, as it was called on the island— something I'd tried a few times before but never really enjoyed. Adam promised me that the marijuana was different on Hawaii, mellow and relaxing. "It will calm down that stomach of yours," he told me. He was right. It did soothe my stomach, but I still didn't love the feeling of getting high. It made me self-conscious. I felt hungry and dimwitted and paranoid about my hunger and dimwittedness. My studio condo was littered with boxes of Cap'n Crunch, a dietary staple of Adam's. We ate it dry, by the handful.

We took a hit to start the day, shared a joint as we explored the Jurassic jungles of Hana, got stoned before snorkeling over kaleidoscope coral reefs, where we glided and dived to the music of whale songs, aching and alien in the distance. *This is what life would be like if I were a pothead,* I thought without irony, as if that weren't the life I was living. On Maui, I often felt as if I were watching a theatrical performance of my life from the last row of a distant balcony, observing this carefree and freewheeling girl played by me.

What would my mother think of this life? I wondered over and over again, and I tried not to care.

I knew Malabar was having a difficult time coping without me, and I felt guilty for not being more supportive. Still, I did not try to be in closer touch. One call per week was what I'd promised her, and one call was all I could give. However unsuitable Adam might have been, I was in love, a first for me, and through that surrender, I achieved genuine emotional distance from Malabar. Plus I was having fun. Whatever pent-up teenage energy had been thwarted in me because of my role in my mother's affair was now rushing the gate. At last, I was the one experimenting with sex, drugs, and adventures. I was the one having the time of my life.

One morning over coffee on my deck, the first joint of the day already stubbed out in an ashtray, Adam bluntly asked me what I was escaping from.

"Escaping?" The question took me by surprise.

I couldn't see the ocean from my condo, but I could hear it, and the rhythm of the waves lapping at the shore made it seem like the world itself was breathing.

"Everyone comes here to get away from something," he said matter-of-factly.

"You first," I said.

"Factory life." I already knew this. Adam had grown up in Ozaw-kie, Kansas, and dropped out of high school at age sixteen to join his father and brother at a printing factory. The money had been good but the monotony and chemicals unbearable.

I thought about my own life so far: prep school, Cape Cod, an Ivy League education on the horizon. The privilege of it all embarrassed me. What could I possibly be escaping? My brain, fuzzy with THC, came up with nothing. I didn't know how to answer the question.

Adam refilled our coffee cups, lit a cigarette, waited.

A puffy cumulus cloud towed its shadow across the lawn below us, and as I followed the dark spot racing along the ground, the story of my mother and Ben spilled from my mouth. It was a relief to talk openly about my secret. Let me be clear: I did not actually believe that my mother's affair was why I was living on Maui. Nevertheless, I was telling Adam Malabar's story — our story, really — and I channeled a boundless tide of moments and emotions into an abridged narrative: the kiss, the exotic meals, the constitutionals. And the lies. So many lies. When I got to the end, when the words finally stopped forming, my hands had become a wedge clenched tightly between my thighs.

"Holy shit!" Adam said, letting out a long, low exhale.

Not the reaction I expected.

"Holy shit," he repeated. "What kind of person would—"

Would what? I wondered. I wasn't following.

"What kind of person would do that to her daughter? And with her husband's best friend? Jesus Christ. Your mother sounds like a piece of work."

I felt confused, suddenly thrust into a state of disequilibrium. Adam was getting this all wrong. He saw Malabar as perpetrator, not victim. I must have failed to relate the complexities of the situation, I decided. But how to explain the tragedies of my mother's life when words were inaccessible? I was so stoned.

"You've misunderstood," I said, the sensation of anger rising within me. "It's not like that."

I dived into the details and tried to explain that Charles and Lily were both ill, not at all the spouses that the others deserved. Ben and my mother were, in fact, doing the honorable thing by staying with their respective partners. "Not everyone would," I assured him. "I don't think Charles would survive for five minutes without my mother." I let that sink in. "He's completely dependent on her. And my mother loves him. Really, she does. She's still really good to him. She takes care of all his needs."

As I spoke, a memory swam to the surface.

I was seven, and my mother, Peter, and I were visiting Charles in the hospital, where he was recovering from his strokes, trying to regain speech and mobility on his right side. His face lit up in a lopsided smile at the sight of my mother, his great love, his betrothed. We had made his favorite cookies the night before, had rolled out and cut the dough, sprinkled the circles with cinnamon sugar. Now my mother was placing them, three in a row, on the rolling hospital table tucked against Charles's belly.

"You can have as many as you want," she told him, "provided you use your right hand."

Determination transformed Charles's features. After two weeks of hospital food, he wanted one of Malabar's treats. He lifted his semi-paralyzed right arm over the target, lowered his hand onto the cookie, and dragged it to the edge, where it teetered precariously as he tried to grip it with a thumb that was no longer fully opposable. Cookie after cookie fell onto his chest and belly. My mother kept placing new ones on the table, and Charles kept trying and failing to grab them. Finally, exhausted from the exertion and clearly frustrated, Charles let his right arm drop onto his lap, where his hand landed on a fallen cookie. He smiled. Instead of trying to grasp it, he scooped it with his palm and plowed it up his belly and chest to his outstretched tongue. I still remember Charles's victorious expression and how we cheered.

As I described the scene to Adam—proof of my mother's love for Charles, proof of her deep humanity—I recalled the helpless-looking bumps of Charles's feet under the hospital sheet. The thought of them, those two ghosts, made me tear up. Why on earth was I crying? I looked down. The story had gotten away from me.

"Trust me," I said, regaining my composure. "Neither Ben nor my mom ever intended to fall in love with each other. My mother would never do anything to hurt Charles. Never. She cares about him so much."

Adam stared at me blankly.

"You can't control who you fall in love with, can you," I said, repeating my mother's well-worn phrase.

"I guess not," Adam said, granting me that. But he gave me a curious look, one that in my paranoid state I took to be a judgment on my very DNA, all those chromosomes tethered to Malabar. "But you don't have to *act* on those feelings. And you can certainly draw the line when kids are involved."

I wanted to slap him.

"And exactly who are you to take the moral high ground here?" I asked my drug-dealing boyfriend. I felt an unbearable sense of disloyalty to my mother. Adam knew nothing about Malabar's lonely childhood or how it felt to have her beloved first child die before her eyes, not to mention what it must have been like for her to watch Charles, the love of her life, go from vibrant to elderly overnight. My mother deserved happiness more than anyone I knew.

Adam started to speak, but I interrupted him. "Just forget it. Forget we ever had this conversation. You're getting this all wrong, and I'm done talking about it with you."

"I'm sorry," Adam said, realizing how wrong things had gone. He reached for my arm, but I pulled it away. "I didn't mean to upset you. I've never heard anything like this before. I don't know how to talk about it or how to help you," he said, backpedaling. The look on his face was sincere. "I don't know your folks, but I know that no one's story is simple. And no single story tells the whole truth. I don't understand their problems and I'm sure they wouldn't understand mine."

An understatement if ever there was one.

Adam plucked a ripe papaya from the tree beside our balcony and took it inside, giving me a few minutes to collect myself. He returned and lowered a plate in front of me, the papaya sliced in half, glassy orange, the black seeds scooped out. A peace offering.

"I'm sorry, babe."

I studied the fruit. "Can we just forget we ever had this conversation?" I asked.

"What conversation?" And with that conspiratorial question, his whole face lit up, his eyes crinkling with relief.

I felt a deep sting of affection for him. We'd made it safely to the other side of our first fight. It was as if I were standing outside of time and place. I had nowhere to go, nothing to do, no one to take care of. I ate a spoonful of papaya, which tasted earthy and ripe, like morning breath, only sweet. The light was beautiful; the coffee strong. Gone was my need to understand what mattered and what motivated people. With Adam, I felt moments of contentment I'd never previously known.

———

When I decided to leave Hawaii for the rest of my haphazard adventure, Adam opted to tag along. For the better part of six months, Adam and I cruised the contiguous states, exploring one natural wonder after the next: the Garden of the Gods in Colorado, Carlsbad Caverns in New Mexico, Grand Canyon National Park in Arizona. In postcards to friends and family, I wrote that Adam and I were intrepid travelers, wanderers who were studying life in America. Hell, we were practically anthropologists.

My journals revealed something closer to the truth: We were every bit as aimless and undirected as we'd been in Maui, arriving at landmarks and monuments as often by accident as by intention. We stayed in highway motels, played pool in grungy bars, followed dubious people into back alleys to buy weed. Daily, I placed myself in situations a hairsbreadth away from real danger, some part of me embracing the notion that a misstep could chart my future as much as college ever would. And it was the tension between wanting to escape my old life and getting caught in my new one that kept me careening from one small town to the next in search of God knows what.

My mother and I spoke every Sunday afternoon. The second I heard the delight in her voice — "Rennie!" — I was right back in Massachusetts with her, immediately drawn into the familiar intimacy, intoxicated by the secrets and hidden perils of her life. Despite all my risky behavior, Malabar's affair still had me beat for excitement, still gave me the biggest rush. Her antics were more thrilling than anything that ever happened to me on the road. Plus, no matter how far from her I was, when things got bad my mother turned to me for advice. I lived for the adrenaline kick of those moments. With Malabar, I was still the accomplice, the girl behind the wheel of the getaway car, revving the engine outside the bank, ready to drop it into gear as soon as she came running.

"We had a close call this week," my mother said quietly into the phone. "You would have died. Ben and I were in the pantry kissing, and out of nowhere, Lily materialized in the doorway behind him."

"Tell me everything," I said. I could picture the scene right down to the angle of my mother's body, how she likely steadied herself with a hand on the shelf where she kept the pasta. I might as well have been in the pantry with them.

"I don't think she saw the kiss," my mother said, "but Ben's hands were definitely holding my face."

"Jesus," I said and took a deep breath, trying to slow my racing heart. "What did you do?"

"Well, if you can believe it, I froze," my mother said. "But Ben was brilliant. He tilted my head up and told Lily I had something in my eye. 'You're blocking the light, Lily,' he said to her. I mean, Rennie, the man had the gall to sound irritated." My mother laughed.

"And then what?"

"He told her to find some eye rinse and she scooted off to do his bidding. You know Lily. Such an obedient wife," my mother said contemptuously.

"What about Charles?" I asked. The pantry was just fifteen feet from where he must have been sitting.

"Oh, Charles was fine. He's always buried in a book. He didn't see a thing."

I wondered what he might have heard. "Why can't you guys hold off until you're alone?" I asked sternly. "Seriously, Mom."

"A fire needs air, sweetheart," my mother said. "Besides, I'm getting tired of waiting. I need out of this life." And then, after a long pause, she added, "I miss you. I wish you'd come home."

From the pay phone, I looked across the road at Adam. Leaning against the car in worn blue jeans and old T-shirt, his hair disheveled, a Marlboro Red hanging from his lips, my boyfriend looked like a blond James Dean, only grimier. He was twenty-five to my eighteen, a high-school dropout who hadn't held a real job in years, a smalltime drug dealer.

At least I wasn't looking to be rescued like my mother was, I thought. Adam didn't have money, prestige, or even the slight promise of a future, and yet I was in love with him. The very idea of this made me feel superior to Malabar, made me think that I was capable of a purer kind of love. *Adam can offer me nothing. Proof that I'm in this for love,* I wrote in my journal that night.

My mother and Ben were more than three years into their affair, and neither of their spouses seemed the worse for it. A few months earlier, however, it had been discovered that Charles had a brain aneurysm. "A ticking time bomb" was how my mother described it. But as the surgery was risky, she and the doctors had opted to wait and monitor it. Charles was not told. At some point, the aneurysm would become too large to ignore, but for now, my stepfather remained unchanged—weakened from his strokes, but still vibrant in his own ways. And Lily's decline, if it could be described as such, was barely discernible. If those radiation pellets, now forty years in her chest, were ravaging her organs, there was scant external evidence—except for her voice, of course, ever scratchier and weaker. No one's death appeared to be imminent, that was for sure, and my mother's patience for the long game was wearing thin.

"I'll be home soon, Mom," I promised.

"Good," she said. "Remember, we are two halves of one whole. I'm not complete without you. I need my best friend back."

I looked at Adam, who had opened a map and spread it out on the hood. I wondered where we'd spend the night. I longed for a strong drink, the kind my mother would make to take the edge off, something that would burn going down, loosen my limbs and cloud my mind.

NINE

I WAS EIGHTEEN when I returned home to Cape Cod in July of 1984, slightly over a year after I'd left. Despite the intentional distance I'd put between my mother and me, when I drove up and saw her waiting for me on the back porch, I scrambled out of the car without turning the motor off, forgetting about Adam in the passenger seat. I fell into her arms and rested my head on her shoulder, where time collapsed and I felt the ineffable sense of being home and in a safe and familiar sanctuary.

"Please don't ever do that again, Rennie. I felt like I was missing a limb without you," my mother whispered, planting kisses all over my face, on my cheeks and nose and forehead. "A whole year? What were you possibly thinking?"

"I've missed you so much, Mom."

I was relieved to find that we still fit together in the exact same way. At five feet eight inches, I had reached my final height, but my mother remained an inch taller, so her arms wrapped around my shoulders and mine fit snugly below, around her waist. In this way, she was still the mother, the one who held, and I was still the child, the one being held.

"Are things going okay?" I asked, my arms still around her. I didn't want to let her go. "How's Charles? Have you been getting enough time with Ben?"

Her body shifted, became heavier.

"It keeps getting harder," she said, her voice catching. "Some days I have trouble believing that it will ever work out."

It had been four years since Ben first kissed my mother, fifteen hundred days, thirty-five thousand hours. For more than twelve million minutes, my mother had been desperately in love with someone she wasn't sure she would ever have. She walked the fine line between projection and possibility, hoping against hope.

"It'll be okay, Mom," I said, giving her a final tight squeeze before we released each other. "I just know it will. You and Ben deserve each other."

"You always say just what I need to hear, Rennie. Thank you," she said, taking a step back and looking at the whole of me. I imagined that I looked pretty much as I always had, blond and healthy, perhaps a few pounds heavier from a diet of roadside-diner food.

Adam came over to say an awkward hello to my mother, whom he'd met during a brief visit we made to Boston to collect my car. She'd been unimpressed by him then and looked equally unenthusiastic about him now. "Why don't you unpack the car," I said to him, squeezing his arm.

My mother and I settled on a bench on the porch and picked up as if no time had passed. She caught me up on Peter and Charles and then leaned in. "Now, don't be mad at me, sweetie," she said, "but I confided in a few more people while you were gone. I just had to. I was going crazy without you here. I needed someone to talk to."

My alarm was instantaneous. Malabar had promised she wouldn't let her secret go beyond me and her best friend, Brenda. We both knew the potential dangers of widening that circle.

I felt a familiar tightness gather in my gut, a stomachache forming. "What? What do you mean? Who else knows?"

My mother started ticking off the names: Deborah, her college roommate; Matt, a former colleague from Time-Life Books; Rachel, a friend in San Francisco; Nancy, a neighbor in Chestnut Hill; Steven, an old boyfriend; Suzanne, her cousin . . .

I put up my hand for her to stop.

My mother's and Charles's lives had changed while I was on the road. They had moved out of 100 Essex and into the top two floors of a townhouse on Beacon Hill that, fortunately for Charles, had an elevator. Although Charles was only in his mid-sixties, he seemed at least a decade older, his walk now a permanent shuffle, his brain aneurysm a looming threat, although he still hadn't been told about it. If left untreated, the aneurysm would eventually rupture, killing him instantly. But his weak heart made surgery extremely dangerous. It was a lose-lose situation.

My mother had hired a caregiver named Hazel to look after Charles in Boston, giving her the autonomy to go to Cape Cod or sneak off to see Ben. Hazel was middle-aged, from Nova Scotia, and, according to my mother, dreary and jowly.

"She's a simpleton, really, Rennie," my mother complained. "But there aren't a lot of people who want part-time work. It's fine. And Charles doesn't mind her. We only need her for a couple of hours a day to tidy and cook."

—

My brother eyed me warily at our reunion and I became aware of a new distance between us. Peter had been transformed while I was away. He'd had a final growth spurt that catapulted him above six feet, ensuring that he would forever tower over me. He'd gone from boy to man and had a potent arsenal of new gestures, not to mention considerable charm, which he would very occasionally direct toward me. Like our father, Peter had a way with beautiful women, some of whom were my friends.

My stepfather, Charles, gave me a warm welcome and was sweet as ever, but his handsome face, more deeply lined than I remembered, looked distressed. He seemed to have sunk further into the world of his curiosities and was especially obsessed with the *Whydah,* that ghost of a shipwreck that had captured his imagination. In 1717, the ship was caught in a treacherous nor'easter off Cape Cod and went down. For years, the three of us — Malabar, Peter, and I — had listened unenthusiastically to our resident armchair treasure hunter as he waxed on about the pirates who'd captured the ship on its maiden voyage and about the spoils aboard that had been lost at sea. He had theories as to where the ship had sunk and how the tides might have moved the loot. He read book after book about it and shared details he thought might ignite some passion in us, but to no avail. We found his obsession charming yet easy to ignore. After all, treasure hunters, salvagers, and "mooncussers" — land-based pirates who plundered ships that ran aground on dangerous coasts at night — had been chasing this dream for more than two hundred and fifty years. Surely if there had been treasure to find, it would have been found already.

Neither Charles nor my mother put forth much effort to make Adam feel at home; it was as if they knew he wouldn't be around for long and was not worth the investment. But Adam was also stand-offish; he wanted no part of the everyday lies and silences that had become second nature to me. Within a few weeks of Adam's and my arrival, my mother suggested that Adam rent his own place.

"It's one thing to shack up on the road, Rennie; it's another thing to do so under my roof," Malabar said, insisting she worried about what the neighbors might think.

The request to modify our living arrangement came as a relief to Adam. He had gotten a job as a dishwasher, and as soon as he got his first paycheck, he rented a dilapidated one-room cottage on Crystal Lake, just a few miles away, where peepers and frogs chorused nightly and lilies broke open each morning. I split my remaining time on Cape Cod alternating between two homes and two families, something I'd been doing my whole life, and waitressing at one of the more popular seafood restaurants in town, Sally's Clam Bar.

Over the course of the summer, things cooled with Adam. We struggled to get along, but our differences were too stark on my home turf. And although we were heartbroken, we were both strangely eager for August to roll around, for me to leave for college in New York, for our relationship to get to its final resting place.

—

A few days before I left for college and made what I imagined would be my permanent escape, the Southers came for an end-of-the-summer *Wild Game* test weekend. They had been meeting regularly while I was traveling and were compiling their successful recipes. My mother's best friend, Brenda, was also visiting. Brenda was the first person after me to learn about Ben. Like me, she had become enmeshed, regularly meeting Malabar and her lover for drinks at the InterContinental in New York City, the hotel where Ben and Malabar stayed during their trysts. Brenda had known my mother since they'd worked together at Bloomingdale's in their early twenties. She had been a bridesmaid at Malabar's wedding to my father and had supported my mother through the dissolution of that marriage after she met Charles.

I was on the back porch scanning the reading requirements for Columbia's core curriculum and daydreaming about lofty dorm-room discussions of *The Iliad* and *The Symposium* when I heard the Southers pull into our driveway. As soon as I put down the college pamphlet, Ben bounded up the steps and enveloped me in a bear hug.

"We missed you, Rennie," he said, and I understood that "we" did not refer to himself and his wife. Ben considered me an integral part of his affair with my mother, a secret second daughter.

Lily gave me a peck on the cheek. "Good to see you home in one piece," she said. "Your mother must be over the moon."

I took in Lily's appearance, searching for any indication that her health might be declining. Was she frailer than when I'd seen her last? She looked birdlike and brittle but no worse than before, as far as I could tell. Then I realized what I was doing and felt my face grow hot with shame.

I led the Southers through the house to the opposite porch, the front one facing the bay, where Charles and my mother were sitting at the table underneath the large umbrella. Brenda, who wore clothes that covered her pale skin from head to toe, occupied herself deadheading the flowering plants that ran along the bench on the wraparound deck.

"How do!" Ben called, announcing his presence long before he got to the screen door.

When Ben reached Brenda, he lifted the brim of her enormous hat and gave her a quick kiss. "Brenda, throw this God-awful thing out and get some sun," he said. "You look like a ghost."

"Brenda, please ignore him," Lily said cheerily. "He's incorrigible."

Charles sighed as he stood. He acknowledged his old friend with a left-handed handshake but looked past him to Lily, whom he greeted warmly. "Good to see you, Lily," he said and then gestured for everyone to sit before sinking heavily back into his own chair.

My mother brought out a tray with long stirring spoons and six tall glasses filled with ice and garnished with fresh mint and lemon wedges. She poured freshly brewed tea into each glass and offered everyone a choice of simple syrup or Sweet'n Low.

"Well, this sure feels like old times," Ben said, wrapping his large hand around my knee. He took a sip of tea. "I can't tell you how happy we are to have you back in our clutches."

The rose hips and honeysuckle bushes that grew wild along the bank above the beach nodded in the breeze. The tide was ebbing, and the constantly shape-shifting sandbars inched their way toward the water's surface. The channel had changed in the year that I was away. Now at low tide, the lobster boats had to swing in a wide loop to avoid the shallows instead of passing directly across. Just five years earlier, when my mother renovated our living room, she'd had a special wall of sliding glass doors placed facing northward to frame the spectacular spot where the ocean slashed through the beach and spilled into our harbor. But in a dazzling disregard of Malabar's renovation, nature had moved the ocean's cut northward and taken with it my mother's perfect view.

"Our test nights weren't quite the same without you," Ben continued. "Now, where's this young gentleman who seems to have stolen your heart? When do I get to meet him?"

Apparently, Malabar hadn't told Ben that Adam's and my relationship was on the rocks. Unsure how my mother had presented the situation, I demurred. "He's working today."

"Too bad," Ben said. "He's a lucky guy to have found you, but you tell him from me, just one misstep"—he pantomimed the wringing of a neck, the gesture he'd used that very first night to show how he killed the pigeons—"and he's done for." Ben smiled, took a large sip of tea, and winked at me. "Besides, I've had someone in mind for you for quite some time. I've just been waiting for you to hit eighteen."

I blushed. Who could he mean?

"Ben," my mother said, changing the subject. "I couldn't help but notice that you've arrived empty-handed. Exactly what are we testing this weekend? The air?"

Ben laughed; he'd been waiting for this moment. "Well, with Rennie back and Brenda visiting, I thought we'd be up for a new challenge. What do you think of an eat-what-you-kill weekend?"

Brenda's mouth popped open in surprise. Born in New Jersey and raised in Manhattan, she was a city girl if ever there was one. When she wasn't in gardening gloves to prune my mother's bushes, her fingers were festooned with chunky silver rings. She would not be using her lovely soft hands as tools to dig clams from the mud or rip mussels off rocks, and Ben knew this.

"Now, darling," Ben said to my mother, hamming it up. "What is your pleasure? Lobster? Striped bass? Mussels? Cherrystones? Your wish is my command, as always."

I studied Charles during this bold exchange—had Ben always

been so overtly flirtatious? — and noticed a half smile on the left side of my stepfather's mouth. Our eyes met, and Charles held my gaze. In that moment, I felt sure of it: He knew. Or, at the very least, he suspected. He looked down suddenly and shook his head. *Did he know that I knew?*

"I've got it," Malabar said gamely. "I'd like some whitebait for the cocktail hour tonight. And tomorrow I'll whip up a bouillabaisse with whatever else you catch."

"Malabar, you are a whiz," Lily said.

"Done and done," Ben said.

———

In a corner of our basement, my mother and I pulled weathered beach chairs, threadbare windbreakers, broken fishing rods, and other detritus from a pile of forgotten paraphernalia underneath which we thought we might find our old whitebaiting net.

"I think Ben and I should go whitebaiting alone," I said. "You need to stay home with Charles and Lily this afternoon. Charles seems off. Something's wrong."

"Nonsense. I want to go," my mother said. "Brenda can entertain those two."

"Mom, did something happen that you haven't told me about? Does Charles know?" I asked. My panic felt physical, like something lodged in my chest.

"Of course not," she said, tugging at a Styrofoam surfboard. "Charles doesn't *know* anything." Behind the surfboard was the net. "Voilà!"

A twelve-foot-long, three-foot-high rectangle of netting was leaning against the corner, neatly rolled around two tall end poles. We unfurled it to check for holes and rot, but despite its having sat unused in our damp basement for several years, the net seemed to be in good shape. We rolled it back up until our fingers met. I placed my pointer finger over hers and pressed down. "I hope you're right, Mom."

My mother handed me her pole and began to put things back in the pile.

"Charles seems depressed," I said. "I think he's onto you two."

"Rennie, has it ever occurred to you that you don't know everything? Charles is depressed because he's worried about his health."

"I thought he didn't know about the aneurysm," I said.

"He doesn't. But that doesn't mean he's unaware that he's in poor health. It's dreadful to get old. You were probably too young to remember how different Charles was before his strokes." Her back was to me and she busied herself with organizing the beach junk. "Facing your own mortality is terrifying."

"Mom, stop. Can you look at me, please?"

She faced me and I saw fear. It occurred to me for the first time that perhaps my mother was afraid of Charles dying. Perhaps it was the thought of being left alone — of being widowed at such a young age — that had driven her into Ben's arms in the first place. I knew she had genuinely loved Charles when they first met and that she still cared for him now.

"You and Ben are more obvious than you realize. I see things a bit more clearly, having been gone for so long. I'm telling you, Charles suspects. Please be more careful," I begged. "And please, please do not tell anyone else. Too many people know already."

"Well, if you hadn't gone rogue on me, gallivanting all over the place," my mother said, attempting humor, "I wouldn't have had to find new confidants."

"Stop," I said again. "I'm worried. Charles is not an idiot. You need to think about his feelings."

"Fine," she said. "Go whitebait without me."

⚊

Ankle-deep in warm water, Ben and I stretched the net, each holding a pole, and pulled it taut. The bottom of the weave was studded with small weights, the top with floats. We walked out a few feet until the water came to our thighs, and then I anchored my pole in the sand, holding it at the base, so one shoulder dipped low and my head tilted sideways, my cheek skimming the surface of the water. Ben, also hunched over, scraped his pole along the sandy bottom, making a large arc around me, the net billowing out from us like a sail.

He traveled a bit more than 180 degrees and said, "Ready."

On the count of three, we flipped our poles parallel to the water's surface and scooped up the net, raising hundreds of minnows as the ocean spilled out. The ensnared fish flopped helplessly, tiny gills snapping open and shut. We made our way back to shore, where we'd left a bucket filled with ocean water.

"Spectacular catch," Ben said, delighted. He dropped to his knees and started separating the silver-sided whitebait from the ordinary chum, placing the former in the bucket and tossing the latter over his shoulder, back into the bay. "You just never know what's lurking beneath the surface."

"Ben, I need to ask you something." I had grown more confident in the year away. My voice was strong and did not waver.

He nodded for me to continue but didn't look up, fully absorbed in his task.

"Does Charles know about you and Mom?"

Ben's rhythm shifted and he slowed down, possibly giving himself time to consider my question. When his sorting was done, he rose to his feet and hauled the empty net back to the water, motioning for me to join him. I did and we stretched the net to its full length and flipped it over, dunking each side into the harbor to remove stray strands of seaweed.

"The truth is," Ben said slowly, "he confronted me in the spring."

My heart sank. "What made him suspicious?"

"He didn't say," Ben said, shrugging. "He must have just sensed something."

We walked back to shore.

"I denied it, of course. And Charles believed me, I'm sure of that." Ben plucked off some bits of brown mung as he rolled his end of the net toward me. "In fact, after that, he felt bad for asking and apologized. It's not exactly a small accusation."

I took this in. Ben was wounded that his best friend could have come to such a terrible conclusion, and Charles felt guilty for having made the accusation. Both men knew the truth but fervently preferred the lie.

"Did you tell Mom about it?"

Ben shook his head.

Peter came up behind us with a close friend of mine whom he'd started dating. They were headed out for an afternoon marsh ride and later to a cookout and bonfire on the outer beach.

"What did you catch?" my friend asked, peering into the bucket. We acted as if there were nothing unusual about her having plans with Peter that didn't include me.

"Whitebait," I said. "Ever had them?"

Her nose wrinkled. "They're so small. How do you clean them?"

"You don't. You eat them whole—guts, head, bones, and everything. Nauset French fries," Peter answered for me. Then, eager to get on the water, he said, "Let's go."

I watched as they clambered first into my brother's dinghy and then onto his boat, Peter at the stern, my friend in the fore. I wondered if Peter, too, had guessed about my mother and Ben. That might explain why he'd been more distant than usual since I got home, speaking to me in monosyllables, some low-grade resentment always simmering beneath the surface.

I sank down onto the sand, feeling impossibly alone. Why wasn't I going to this bonfire with friends? Or out with Adam, who'd invited me to see Panama, the Judge, and the Preacher play at the Woodshed—my favorite local band, my favorite local bar. Instead, I'd opted to stay home and help my mother, and this was the first time I'd become aware of a lacuna between the life I was living and the one I wanted to live. I no longer understood the point of the charade. Everyone, it seemed, was in on Malabar's secret. Brenda for sure. Adam, though that was my fault. Possibly Peter. And now, worst of all, Charles—although apparently, he'd chosen to accept his friend's denial for the sake of maintaining his own dignity. Was Lily the only one still in the dark?

I'd be leaving for college in just a few days, I reminded myself. My next escape would come soon enough.

Behind me, Ben was already halfway up the bank of stairs to our house, bucket in one hand, net in the other. In a few minutes, he'd be showing Malabar our catch, all those whitebait frantically darting around the pail, and her reaction would be pure delight. This was my mother's favorite kind of dish to prepare, simple and dramatic. As soon as the cocktail hour was under way, she'd swirl hot oil and butter around a skillet. Then she'd grab a fistful of still-wriggling minnows, coat them in seasoned flour, and sprinkle them evenly around the sizzling-hot pan, where they'd curl into crispy, golden Cs. Speed was key—whitebait were best served piping hot with salt.

Out on the water, Peter lowered his motor and yanked hard on the pull cord; the engine sputtered to life. His boat, a canary-yellow skiff that he'd bought when he was fourteen, was his most prized possession. He maneuvered it carefully through the moorings and past the low-wake zone to the channel, then he accelerated. My brother was a beautiful sight, with his muscular legs set apart, one foot slightly forward for balance, his knees bent to absorb impact, leaning his body into the turns, feeling the tug of the current beneath his feet through the metal of the skiff's hull. Something shifted inside of him when he was on the water. He seemed to stand outside of time, lost to it, completely free and at peace.

As my brother sped off without looking back—raced away from me, from our mother, from all the crazy machinations going on in our home—my old friend waved, her fingers waggling absurdly. I felt a pang of envy that somehow Peter had succeeded where I'd failed. He'd put a healthy distance between himself and the madness. He'd managed to grow up, get the girl, and move on, whereas I remained stuck in the scrum of our childhood.

Then Peter's boat turned, and the afternoon sun glinted off its wake, illuminating the skiff from behind—and there it was, a single, powerful word emblazoned in bold black letters across the stern: M A L A B A R.

I waded out into the bay, past the clumps of eelgrass where crabs scuttled away and starfish clung to rocks, until I reached the drop-off. There, I took a huge breath and dived down to the hard bottom. Whatever the surface conditions, it was always calmer below. The water pressed against my ears, creating an insistent silence. I crossed my legs and tried to sit on the ocean floor, a game I'd played since childhood. I fanned my hands and released the air from my lungs to combat my buoyancy, a losing battle. As I felt myself tilt and start to ascend, I kicked off the ground and surged toward the surface. *I'll be gone from here soon*, I thought, shooting through the billow of my hair toward the sunlight.

TEN

I ARRIVED AT COLUMBIA in the fall of 1984 ready to start life anew. My relationship with Adam had reached its logical conclusion, and although he'd show up in New York a couple of times, he soon headed home to Kansas. At college, I intended to create a whole new identity for myself, to obtain some distance from the girl I used to be, a girl so consumed by her mother that she hardly knew where her mother ended and she began.

College was going to be about me. I would apply myself academically and excel. I'd had my year off in which I'd had a few adventures and some gained perspective, but as soon as I'd returned home, I'd gotten sucked right back into the same old patterns. Not again. This time, I would figure out what and who I wanted to be and start that grand life in earnest. I ached to find out what was in store for me. No more people-pleasing. No more running loops on my mother's track, waiting for her to thwack the baton into my hand. In college, the past would be the past, and I would get a fresh start.

Malabar helped me move into my room on the eleventh floor of John Jay Hall on a hot August morning. We unpacked my bags and organized the tiny rectangular area with its narrow bed, standard desk, dime-size sink, and single window facing 114th Street from where I could hear a steady stream of ambulances screaming toward St. Luke's Hospital. The neighbor in the room to my right was a long-haired Trinidadian boy whose main décor was a poster of three girls in thong bikinis photographed from behind, their buttock cheeks sand-dusted to perfection, lined up as if in prayer before an aquamarine ocean. Across the hall, a raucous Texan girl with bangs that were sprayed straight up had a matching comforter and sheet set and towels in complementary colors. And a few doors down, a grim young man sporting army fatigues kept his room completely bare.

My room defied category. From home, my mother had brought a small oriental rug, a standing lamp with a bell-curved shade and a brass knob finial, and an oil painting of a Cape Cod scene: a fishing boat grounded at low tide. We made up the bed with worn floral sheets and covered them with a hand-stitched antique quilt that sported blocky orange tulips with green stems, an estate-sale find. The room looked like an extension of my grandmother's home, some forgotten maid's quarters or an unfinished office.

"Shall we grab an early bite?" my mother asked, smoothing the quilt over the mattress. Although exhausted, she was not prepared for this day to end or to return to her empty nest and elderly husband. She'd already made plans to spend the night with Brenda, who lived close by on the Upper West Side, and then travel back to Massachusetts in the morning to check on Charles. Malabar sensed my hesitation to go with her. The rest of the kids on my floor were planning to order pizza and eat in the common room.

"Really, Rennie? Would a last dinner with me kill you?" My mother ticked off all she'd done for me that day: schlepping me to New York City; buying hangers, an extension cord, a plastic bucket for me to tote my shampoo down the hall to the bathroom; helping me set everything up. "You have the rest of the year to spend with these strangers," she said. Then she softened. "I'm sorry. I'm just missing you already."

We found an Indian restaurant on Broadway. It looked questionable, with a cartoon Ganesh on the side of a threadbare awning, but we decided it had potential. When the waiter appeared to take our order, my mother told him she'd been raised in Bombay and Delhi and could handle real heat. "We want an authentic experience. As hot as the chef can make the vindaloo is how we'd like it," she said.

Not me, I thought, imagining the stomachache that would follow. I studied the bread options: naan, roti, puri.

Then Malabar ordered a power pack in her usual rapid-fire staccato: "A dry Manhattan. Straight up. With a twist. No ice. No fruit." When the waiter tilted his head quizzically, Malabar exhaled her annoyance and repeated the order at exactly the same speed. I asked for a Taj Mahal beer.

My eyes started to water at the first bite of lamb. To my satisfaction, perspiration beaded on my mother's upper lip as well.

She gulped down water and we both started to laugh. It was rare for someone to get the better of Malabar in the kitchen. Either the waiter had taken her at her word—that she could handle the heat—or we were being taught a lesson and the entire kitchen staff was having a good laugh. We suspected the latter.

"You seem happy, Mom," I said.

"Well, certainly not at the prospect of losing you again," she said, frowning. "But at least now I'll have a better excuse for all my trips to New York." She took a dainty bite of vindaloo after wrapping the meat in a piece of naan. "I guess things are improving some. Life is so much easier with Hazel on the ground at home. I can do things like this—a night away—without worrying about Charles."

"Does Hazel spend the night when you're out of town?" I asked.

"No. Charles doesn't need that level of help yet," my mother said. "She just gets to the apartment before Charles comes home from work, tidies up, makes dinner, and double-checks that he takes his medications. She's been a lifesaver."

Their new apartment, in Boston proper, was closer to Charles's office than their old one, but it was a more arduous walk uphill from the T at the end of the day. "The truth is, Hazel is as much for me as she is for Charles. Her presence gives me peace of mind. I'd never forgive myself if something happened to him and no one was there to help."

"What does Charles think of her?" I asked.

"Hazel?" My mother puzzled over the question for a moment, as if she'd never considered it. "Hard to say. He tolerates her. It's not as if she's there to be his friend."

"Is she an okay cook?"

My mother shrugged and then smiled. "She is certainly capable of putting a meal on the table. But let's face it, the bar is rather high on the cooking front, isn't it?"

I was looking for some level of reassurance that Malabar didn't seem willing to provide. "Overall, he's okay with the whole thing, right?" I asked.

"You know Charles. He doesn't complain. But honestly, he doesn't have much say in the matter. No doubt he'd prefer I was home every night to take care of him myself, but I just can't do that. I simply can't. I'd go mad." My mother flagged down the waiter and ordered a glass of wine. "Not while you're off doing your own thing again."

I told myself not to take the bait, but I couldn't help it. "Does going to college really count as doing my own thing?" I asked.

"Oh, Rennie, try to have a sense of humor," my mother said. "Let's not split hairs tonight."

A cloud of tension spread and I found myself avoiding eye contact with her. With my fork, I plowed a path through the curry with a chunk of lamb, knowing that my mother hated for people to play with their food. As our dishes were cleared, Malabar asked — more courtesy than question — if I'd mind if she ordered another glass of wine. I told her that I wanted to get back to my dorm, a small assertion of will. That she was irritated was obvious, but she acquiesced and we walked out of the air-conditioned restaurant and into the muggy Manhattan dusk.

Before stepping into her taxi, Malabar hugged me tightly. "Rennie, I know I don't always say it, but I appreciate all you do for me. I'm going to miss you desperately. I love you."

"I love you too, Mom," I said.

She got in the cab and rolled down the window. "Don't ever forget that you and I are two halves of one whole."

I watched the taxi speed off toward Brenda's apartment, less than twenty blocks away. I'd heard somewhere that all the cells in the human body replaced themselves every seven years. If that was the case, I was already almost an entirely different human from the one my mother had woken up at age fourteen. If I wasn't the same self I used to be, I certainly couldn't be half Malabar.

When I got back to my room, I found a gift my mother had left for me on my desk: a small, leather-framed photograph of the two of us. I studied it, having no memory of when it had been taken or who took it. We were standing beside each other on Malabar's deck, both of us leaning forward, vying for the last small slice of afternoon light. My mother had snagged it, of course; her right hand shielded her eyes. Her left arm was slung around me, vanishing behind my back and making it appear that she was missing that limb, like a pine tree bare on one side, competing for sunlight.

ELEVEN

Cᴏʟʟᴇɢᴇ ʟɪꜰᴇ was immediately engaging: I made friends with my hallmates, wrote essays and crammed for tests, and navigated what seemed like biweekly fire drills that left the occupants of our entire dormitory huddled on the quad in the predawn hours.

Then, late one night less than a month into my freshman year, I woke to the phone ringing.

"Rennie," my mother said as soon as I picked up, her voice in a high register that made it clear she was struggling not to cry. I sat up in bed, disoriented. At first I wondered if I was having a bad dream.

"Are you there, Rennie?"

I rubbed my eyes. "Yes, I'm here. What's wrong? Is Charles okay?"

"It's not Charles. Charles is fine," she whispered. "It's me. Oh, darling, I'm in so much trouble."

I waited, listening to her ragged breathing.

"I need your help. I don't know what to do." Then she burst into tears, a rare event, and cried inconsolably for several minutes. "I'm ruined."

"What happened?" I asked. "Whatever it is, I know we can fix it." I felt desperate to reassure her, but I could only hear sobs. "It's going to be okay, but Mom, I can't help you if I don't know what's going on."

"That despicable woman——" she said, anger momentarily puncturing her despair.

"Breathe, Mom. Take three deep breaths."

She inhaled and exhaled, gathering herself.

"Do you mean Lily? Are we talking about Lily?"

"No, no." She started to sob again. "It's Hazel." She could barely speak. "That bitch found out about Ben. And now she's blackmailing me. What a horrible, miserable person. I'm telling you, she's had it in for me since the day she started working for us. And after all I've done for her. Trusting her in my home. Trusting her with my husband."

Adrenaline surged through my body, that old familiar buzz.

"What exactly did Hazel find?" I asked, making my voice sound calm. "What evidence does she have?"

"Does it matter?" Malabar was hysterical. "If I don't come up with ten thousand dollars, she plans to tell Charles and Lily everything. And if I do come up with the money, what guarantee do I have that this nightmare will end there? What will stop her from asking for more?"

I hadn't met Hazel, but clearly she wasn't as dimwitted as my mother had suggested. "It *does* matter. Do you think she actually took something?"

"I don't think so. I don't know! What am I going to do?" Malabar was silent for a spell and then her voice returned, low and determined. "I will not let her take Ben from me. Ben is *everything* to me. Absolutely everything. My life isn't worth living if I lose him."

Even then, as a freshman in college, I still clung to the notion that somehow I was my mother's favorite, more beloved than Peter or Christopher or even Ben. For better or worse, that was who Malabar was to me, the most central and important person in my life, even if I wished it were otherwise. For as long as her love affair had been going on, for me, the "we" had always been my mother and me. Not Ben and Malabar. If Ben was everything to my mother, then what was I? Was I not worth living for too?

"Okay, calm down. Let's think. We can figure this out," I said. "First of all, your life is absolutely worth living. Please don't say stuff like that. It upsets me. Where are you right now?"

"In the kitchen," she whispered.

I pictured my mother sitting on the stool, elbows splayed on the marble countertop. I heard ice cubes clink and the familiar glug of a bottle upturning.

"Go to sleep," I said, realizing how much she must have had to drink already. "I'll figure something out. I promise."

"Oh, Rennie, I love you," Malabar said, the words thick and heavy in her mouth. I knew she would take one final gulp of her drink to knock herself out. Before I could respond, there was a click and then a dial tone.

From there, I knew, my mother would bump her way down the hallway and slip into my bed, as she often did when I was away. I didn't mind. In fact, I took comfort in the idea that she slept there. I almost never did. The new apartment would never be my home. Stashed in the drawer of my bedside table was a container of her sleeping pills. My mother would swallow a couple—part of her chemical lullaby—to ensure that she'd sleep like the dead for the next ten hours, her face surrounded by pillows. I thought of Christopher, the original source of her insomnia. Our shared birthday had just passed. I had turned nineteen and Christopher would've been twenty-three.

After hanging up, I pulled the first all-nighter of my college career. I paced back and forth the length of my short room, approaching the Hazel problem from every angle. If the woman had evidence, we would have to undermine it. If she didn't, we would have to poke holes in her story. Hazel, this caregiver whom I'd never met, had become my enemy. I needed to figure out how to discredit her, show that she was unhinged, envious, greedy.

At four in the morning, an idea appeared, fully formed.

———

Later that day, I called my mother while Charles was at work and had her scour the apartment looking for whatever had tipped off Hazel. I remained with her on the phone while she flipped through the stack of letters crammed into the oval-shaped velvet container on her desk. Nothing. The contents of both of our bedside nightstands. Nothing. The drawers of her dressing table. Nothing.

I thought about the photographs of our family that hung in the hallway: Peter and me growing up on Cape Cod, my mother and Charles on various trips, a few shots of my stepsiblings, grandparents, and other more distant relatives. There was a single shot that included Ben. Taken on the Southers' lawn, the photograph featured an enormous taxidermied crocodile that Ben had killed, a canoe of equal length behind it, and Ben and my mother kneeling next to each other behind that. They were leaning forward, beaming into the camera, their knees no doubt secretly touching. Charles was standing to one side, looking down at his shoes, his expression inscrutable. Lily, presumably, was the photographer. The shot was revealing only if you already knew about the affair. It was an odd choice to exhibit on a family wall, to be sure, but hardly evidence.

"I have a plan, but for it to work, I need to have some idea of what Hazel knows," I said. "Can you think of anything?"

After a long pause, Malabar said, "Oh God, Rennie. I know exactly what Hazel saw."

"What?"

"I can't believe I did something so stupid."

"Mom?"

"Give me a minute," she said.

I heard her put the receiver down and then, a few seconds later, pick up another in a different room.

"You're going to think I'm an idiot."

"No," I assured her, bracing myself. "Just tell me what it is."

"I kept a file."

"A file?" I repeated. "What do you mean? A file on you and Ben?"

I heard a metal drawer slide open and suddenly understood. In my mother's office, beside her desk, was a nondescript three-drawer file cabinet. I knew its contents well. The top drawer held travel- and food-related information—notes for articles Malabar planned to write, clips of her published pieces, pamphlets for resorts where she hoped to vacation. On my most recent visit, my mother had proudly shown me her signed contract with Globe Pequot, the pub- lishing house that was to publish a compilation of her Do-Ahead Dining columns in the coming year. In that same file, she kept her notes and test recipes for *Wild Game.*

I had never bothered much with the second drawer, which held dull financial records—bank statements, real estate appraisals, cop- ies of old tax returns. But the bottom drawer was a gold mine of information. In it were alphabetized files on every member of our family: Christopher—photographs, his birth certificate, the many condolence letters; Charles—their wedding announcement, infor- mation on Plimoth Plantation, his health records; Peter and me, sep- arate files but with similar contents—birth certificates, report cards, childhood drawings, scribbled love letters to our mother. Malabar also kept a file for each of her parents, another for correspondence with friends, and one for unpublished short stories, which I hadn't known she wrote. And at the very back was a hidden file that con- tained the makings of a scrapbook of her love affair with Ben.

"I kept it where I thought it would be impossible for Charles to reach," my mother said. "Not that he would ever snoop."

My mother was right. Charles was not the sort to spy; that wasn't his style. Nor was it possible for him to stoop over or get down on his knees easily.

"It never occurred to me that anyone else would look," she said.

"What's in it?" I willed my voice to conceal my panic.

"Everything," Malabar said.

I heard contents rustling. "InterContinental hotel stationery. Matchbooks from every restaurant we've been to. Cocktail napkins. Amtrak ticket stubs. Delta Shuttle receipts." Then she paused, and I could hear a smile in her voice. "A love note."

"I thought Ben didn't put his feelings on paper," I said.

"I talked him into it exactly once," she admitted. "He used initials, not names. It reads 'M., I love you absolutely. B.'"

I wondered if Hazel had crosschecked the dates of my mother's travel with Ben's various board meetings, which she marked with line drawings of fish in her calendar.

"Anything else?" I asked.

What followed was a silence so long that I thought my mother had put down the receiver.

"Six Polaroids," Malabar finally said. "I promised Ben that I would destroy them, but I never did."

"How bad are they?"

"Very."

So Hazel had seen a full dossier on my mother and Ben's love affair.

"Can you tell if anything is missing?"

"I don't think so," my mother said. I heard paper shuffling. "No. Nothing's missing. It's all here."

—

Our plan was this: My mother would tell Hazel she needed at least a week to get the money together. During that time, we would finalize every detail of our operation. My mother, pretending to be Hazel, would send letters to a handful of married friends who ran in Lily's circle, including Ben's two sisters, alleging that Malabar was having affairs with their husbands. Our hope was that in the tsunami of preposterous accusations of infidelity, the real one would get lost, a ripple in a vast ocean.

I skipped classes for several days.

Over the phone, Malabar and I struggled for the perfect open-ing phrase. We decided that there was no good way to soft-pedal an adultery accusation, so we settled on *I regret to inform you.* Para-graph two varied from woman to woman but essentially introduced specifics and provided a scenario: *Malabar was seen with your hus-band leaving the Four Seasons Hotel . . . There are receipts for a week-end flight to New York . . . A photo of your husband and Malabar was found in her bedside table.* The closing lines required the greatest consideration. Hazel needed to appear to be making her case, but at the same time there had to be a flaw in the scenario she presented, a refutable fact that would undermine the credibility of her accusa-tion. We accomplished this by selecting a date on which we knew the purported lover had an ironclad alibi—a major family occa-sion, such as a birthday or anniversary—that made it impossible for him to have participated in the alleged tryst.

Malabar drafted, redrafted, and polished these letters, imitating Hazel's handwriting. She read them aloud to me over the phone, and if she had any doubts about the final product, she redid the letter. When they were all finished, she tucked them into envelopes and drove around Boston and Cambridge and Newton, mailing each from a different post office.

As the phone calls came in from various shocked friends, I could picture Malabar in her kitchen, leaning against the wall for support as she held the receiver. She would likely be nervous at first, but I knew my mother would find her groove quickly. The plan was for her to act like she'd been fielding these calls for days.

Can you believe it? I imagined Malabar saying as she roped the phone cord around her long, elegant fingers. *I'm so sorry that this caused you even a moment of distress.*

There'd be a pause as the friend asked more questions.

Oh yes. I fired her last week, Malabar would continue earnestly. *But honestly, who knows the extent of the damage?*

And then more back-and-forth.

It's been a nightmare not knowing who else she has written to and who might believe her lies. Clearly, she wants to destroy my reputation, although it's also conceivable that she's just plain crazy.

Finally, with the chitchat over, Malabar would be in a good position to ask for the big favor. Claiming to be overwhelmed by all the damage control she was undertaking — canceling credit cards, reviewing bank statements, fielding all these phone calls — she would ask the friend if she'd mind calling Lily and telling her what had happened, professing concern that Lily might have gotten a letter too. Malabar knew that it would take only a couple such calls for Lily to conclude that if she heard anything from Hazel, it had to be a hoax.

With each phone call, I imagined, my mother would become more and more in her element, exuding confidence and charisma.

It would be funny if only poor Charles weren't so mortified. When I checked her references, no one mentioned that Hazel was as mad as a hatter! Malabar might be laughing. *A dozen lovers, all these dinners and trips . . . how did I manage it all and still produce a weekly column?*

Each of these friends would likely have the same thought: Who but poised and elegant Malabar could handle this disastrous situation with such grace and humor? I imagined they all wanted to be her closest friend, but that coveted position was already mine.

TWELVE

Wɪᴛʜ ʜᴀᴢᴇʟ ᴠᴀɴǫᴜɪsʜᴇᴅ and Lily none the wiser about her husband's affair, the chaotic storm that had been kicked up quickly dissipated, and Ben and my mother's relationship slipped back into a state of quasi-equilibrium.

This was not the case with me.

If previously I'd had a supporting role in my mother's extramarital activities, by masterminding this false-letter-writing campaign, I'd put myself in the director's chair, presiding over the players. The experience had been heady, for sure, risky and thrilling, and it had resulted in raves from the small audience of my mother and Ben, who were floored by my plan and exhilarated by its perfect outcome.

"You were brilliant," my mother told me over drinks at the Inter-Continental.

"Yes," Ben agreed, toasting the success of my scheme. "A chip off the old block!"

Initially, each dollop of praise chemically rewarded my adolescent brain like a hit of dopamine, but I came down from the high quickly. This lie pressed on my conscience differently than the others. I wrote long diatribes full of self-loathing in my journal and took to staring at my reflection in the mirror until I stopped recognizing myself, like when you say a one-syllable word over and over again and it gradually morphs into a meaningless sound. Lying had become a reflex.

I wondered about what might have resulted from all of our false infidelity accusations. Even though the families involved had responded as we'd hoped — sympathetic to Malabar's unenviable situation with a vindictive employee — we'd thrown no small dash of poison into those marital wells. And this latest falsehood was more than merely slanderous; it expanded and complicated the already complex web of people who were tangled in my mother's affair, forcing me to be even more spider-like in my vigilance as I attempted to detect vibrations and disturbances. I had always felt complicit in my mother and Ben's transgression, but now I was an accessory to a more serious crime.

Plus, I had the uneasy feeling that I didn't know the whole story. Could Hazel's motivation really have been as simple as greed? I wanted to know what had happened to her, how it had all gone down, but my mother refused to tell me. I had no idea if the woman had simply slunk off, tail between her legs, and gotten on with her life. I felt sure my mother had exacted some kind of revenge.

When I pressed my mother for details, she refused. "All you need to know is that Hazel is gone from our lives, Rennie. I don't ever want to think about that miserable woman again," she said. "Trust me, it's best that you don't know. Curiosity killed the cat, my curious girl."

I knew all about curiosity's dangers — Icarus and the sun, Pandora's box, Eve and her lust for knowledge. I hated that Malabar was withholding facts and that she had suddenly chosen to exercise her parental authority to protect me now that I was almost twenty. She'd given up that right long ago. We were friends, equals. I had earned my place at the table and deserved to know everything that happened. I had solved this enormous problem for her, after all. But the more insistent and demanding I became, the more adamant Malabar was in her refusal. She wouldn't budge, and, ironically, the biggest fallout from Hazel's extortion attempt turned out to be a yawning rift between us.

A few days went by, followed by a week, then two. The weeks stacked up to form a month, with another close on its heels, and we found ourselves careering toward the brick wall of the holidays. She rarely called me and I rarely called her. When we did speak, our conversations — exceedingly polite and formal — were more painful than our silences.

I opted to stay in New York City for Christmas, a gauntlet I threw down and immediately wished to retrieve but did not. Early into the new year, my mother's friend Brenda invited me over for tea and a catch-up, telling me she had important news from Malabar. Now that Brenda and I lived in the same city, we'd formed a friendship independent of my mother, and I found myself wondering what Brenda thought of my involvement in my mother and Ben's affair. This wasn't the time to bring it up, however; our meeting was the olive branch from Malabar that I'd been waiting for. Missing my mother felt physical, a steady tug on an invisible umbilical cord. Genes were genes and blood was blood, after all. Silence couldn't alter those facts.

"Call your mother immediately," Brenda told me simply when she saw me. "This nonsense has gone on long enough. Malabar needs you."

On the fifteen-block walk from Brenda's apartment back to John Jay Hall, I scanned my brain for what could possibly be going on, worry rising in my chest. It was early February, just a few days past the anniversary of Christopher's death. It was not a date my parents had ever mentioned or one that we acknowledged as a family, but I had memorized it as a child from Christopher's frayed, canvas-covered photo album. Its last page held a single dried red rose and the words *The End — February 2, 1964. With all our hearts, always.*

Whenever I touched that brittle rose — the color long drained from its stem and flower, shards of leaves and petals gathered in the crease of the album — I felt a liminal contact with a woman I hadn't known, the woman who had lived for thirty-four years before I existed. Somewhere during that lifetime, she had written those words, laid that rose on the final page of her dead son's album, and closed the book.

I had touched that rose at least a hundred times and every time, my reaction had been the same: a pricking sensation behind my eyes, a gathering in my throat, a sudden hollowing of my chest that threatened my ability to breathe. As a child, I used to believe that my physical reaction had to do with an otherworldly connection I had with Christopher. We shared a birthday, after all, and I loved to imagine that we were able to cross the divide between the living and the dead through the secret portal of his rose. But now I understood that the connection I had always felt had been with my mother, not Christopher. I regretted my emotional stinginess of the past few months and I told her that immediately when I called her from my dorm room. A détente was reached straightaway, and apologies flowed from both sides. It seemed incomprehensible that we hadn't spoken — really spoken — since October.

Then: "It's Charles," my mother said quietly.

"What about him?" I asked.

Charles's most recent angiogram — a test that involved injecting dye into blood vessels and using x-rays to evaluate blood flow — revealed that the aneurysm in his brain had grown to a critical point. The cardiologist informed my mother that with Charles's weak heart, the necessary surgery was extremely risky, information we already knew. He now gave Charles a fifty-fifty chance of surviving the surgery. Without the operation, the aneurysm would eventually rupture and Charles would die within minutes. Of this, the doctor was 100 percent certain.

"What does Charles think?" I asked after my mother told me this.

"He still doesn't know. The doctors advise strongly against telling him," she said. "And I've decided that they're right. What good would come of it? He wouldn't be able to enjoy his life. He'd be terrified that each and every day might be his last."

I wondered about the wisdom of not telling him. What about giving him a last opportunity to make amends and say goodbye? I would want to know if I were in Charles's situation. Besides, some part of him must already know, I concluded, and I wondered if he was upset by the deception.

"The surgery is scheduled for the fall," she said, sighing deeply. "The hope is that Charles is not in immediate danger and can enjoy a beautiful summer."

"And you'll tell him about this . . . when?"

"In the fall. Please come home as soon as school ends. It might be our last summer with him."

THIRTEEN

CHARLES HAD REASON to feel happy that summer of 1985. His belief that one day the remains of the *Whydah* would be found—a possibility that our family collectively dismissed—had recently been validated when the archaeologist Barry Clifford discovered the wreck not twenty miles from our house and not far from where Charles had long suspected was its final grave. Now there were regular reports of its spoils: sword handles, pieces of eight from the eighteenth century, a whole cannon. All summer long, my stepfather combed the local papers for news, awaiting confirmation of the vessel's identity, which, if found, would make it the first and only pirate shipwreck ever authenticated. With the delight of the vindicated, Charles read aloud articles listing the plunder discovered —rings, spoons, silver and gold coins—and hammered us with *Whydah* facts we already knew: The ship had been on its maiden voyage in 1717 when it was hijacked by pirates after departing Jamaica. The leader was Samuel "Black Sam" Bellamy. The vessel was more than a hundred feet long. It carried African captives in the cargo hold.

"Think of how much treasure the *Whydah* must have had when she went down," my stepfather mused one gorgeous July morning, sipping from a mug of Sanka I'd made. Malabar was not yet awake. "Think about all the vessels she must have ransacked between the Bahamas and here."

I was more curious about the human cargo. "What happened to the slaves when the pirates took over?" I was on the kitchen side of the counter, looking at the lobster boats streaming past as they made their way to the cut.

Charles told me that it was typical for pirates to free a ship's prisoners, some of whom — having nothing to lose — would join their liberators in raising the Jolly Roger. The irony that outlaw buccaneers, presumably morally bankrupt individuals, treated freed slaves as equals on their crew was not lost on me.

But it was the treasure that fascinated Charles. "Just two months after the *Whydah*'s capture, they grounded her on a sandbar and she broke apart in the surf. It was one of those ferocious storms, seventy-mile-an-hour winds. The pirates were probably all drunk." Charles shook his head at their folly. "If Barry Clifford has this right, there might be plunder from over fifty other ships in the vicinity. Think of all that loot — lead shots, doubloons, silver spoons . . ."

"Why do you think the pirate captain sailed all the way up here?" I asked.

"Black Sam?" My stepfather smiled at my naiveté. "Why does any man do something foolish or dangerous? For a woman. For love. Old Samuel Bellamy had a girl waiting for him in Wellfleet."

For the duration of that summer, Charles managed never to utter the phrase *I told you so*. Instead, he let the facts speak for themselves. *Whydah*-laden confetti in the form of articles torn from newspapers littered every end table and armchair in our living room, reminders of what might have been ours had we only listened.

I returned to the job I'd held the previous summer, waitressing at Sally's Clam Bar, serving up ice-cold beers alongside fried clams and steamed lobsters. The food was cooked to order and expensive, and the waitstaff hustled customers in and out quickly, our blue aprons bulging with tips. It was at Sally's that I met Kyra, who would become a lifelong friend.

On Kyra's first day, she pulled into the restaurant's parking lot on a moped and engaged the kickstand with a quick smack of her heel. She shook out her short brown hair, which had a bold streak of silver-gray down the front, and sauntered toward the hostess stand. Kyra looked one part badass and two parts girl-next-door, and her presence struck me as if I were a divining rod and she were water. I felt some internal movement, a shift toward her, and the overwhelming feeling of wanting to be her friend, an emotion the likes of which I hadn't experienced as an adult.

Over the course of the summer, Kyra and I spent our days off on the outer beach, sitting in the dunes and discussing the tangle of our families while watching long blades of grass arch over in the ocean breeze and drawing circles in the sand. To Kyra, I admitted my wildly inappropriate crush on Hank, the boyfriend of our boss, Sally. I told her about how, earlier in the summer, he'd caught me red-handed sneaking a piece of cheesecake in the downstairs walk-in freezer. When Hank ordered me out of the freezer, our arms had brushed, causing an unexpectedly electric response. What followed was one of those strange slow-motion moments, like the kind that allows a parachutist to leap from the hatch. A kiss had been all but inevitable, I told Kyra.

"Don't do it," she warned, as if the decision still lay ahead of me.

"We didn't," I confessed, recalling how Sally's voice had drifted down the stairs and brought us to our senses.

Kyra was the first person I'd known whose complicated family situation rivaled my own; divorced parents, mother living abroad, father absorbed by a new family. I told Kyra everything about myself—all of my lies and duplicities—and, unlike Adam, she listened without judgment. For the first time, I felt heard, understood, less alone.

Toward the end of the summer, Kyra came over to our house for dinner. It was rare for Malabar to include one of Peter's or my friends, and I was nervous. My mother always had an easier time finding fault than strengths in our friends. But Kyra managed to hold her own in every way—with the booze (a power pack to start, of course) and my mother's exotic cooking (mussels, kale, and chorizo in a garlicky broth, delicious but not necessarily to everyone's taste). Kyra made a near-fatal slip early on when she suggested that bitters might improve the cocktail—this was how her father preferred his Manhattans—but recovered quickly, salvaging the moment by turning her attention to my mother's still-life collection. She studied one painting in particular, a recent yard-sale acquisition, of a pint of fresh strawberries tipped over in a patch.

"I love this one, Malabar," Kyra said. "You can practically taste how sweet and succulent those berries are."

I mouthed, *Suck-up.*

Kyra smiled and laid it on even thicker with talk of brushstrokes and reflected light. She was an attentive listener and a captivating conversationalist who felt comfortable enough to talk art and food with Malabar. She regaled my mother with stories of her own culinary specialty, Southern fare—fiddlehead ferns, fried green tomatoes, grits, and other regional delicacies. To my shock, as Kyra got ready to leave, my mother invited her back—a first—and made my new best friend promise to bring a homemade peach and blueberry cobbler.

I walked Kyra to her car, a borrowed VW bug that required hotwiring to start, awed by how she had charmed Malabar.

"Piece of cake," she said. "Your mother's just lonely."

I was dumbfounded. Malabar had dinner parties almost every

weekend; she had been juggling two men for years. "My mother's not lonely," I said.

"You're wrong," said Kyra. "Loneliness is not about how many people you have around. It's about whether or not you feel connected. Whether or not you're able to be yourself."

I was at a loss for words. Was Malabar not being herself when she was being Malabar?

"You know what I mean," Kyra said, breaking it down for me. "The lonely feeling comes from not feeling known."

—

As the long days of summer constricted and the afternoon light grew slanted, announcing that autumn was on the horizon, I felt stricken at the thought of leaving Cape Cod, unsure when I would see Kyra again, scared about Charles's impending procedure, and worried that my mother would fall apart under the stress.

I made a single trip back to Boston that fall, a long weekend in October, with the dual purpose of celebrating my birthday and wishing Charles good luck with his operation. My mother had finally told my stepfather about his condition, though she'd downplayed the gravity of his upcoming surgery. Charles was not brave when it came to facing his illness. He hated to be alone and was openly anxious about the discomfort of hospitals. His fears were justified. We all knew what he'd been through after his strokes, how hard he'd had to fight for months and months.

On the morning I was to return to New York City, my stepfather and I made a pact: We promised each other that we would scour the beaches together the following summer. We were determined to find at least one *Whydah* doubloon or other relic. I hugged him goodbye and told him how much I loved him.

—

I held my breath the day of the surgery, waiting for a call from my mother, which finally came in the afternoon.

"He made it," she said, relief palpable in her voice. "The doctor repaired the aneurysm."

I wept with happiness. "Can I say hello?"

"No, sweetheart. He's still in intensive care. I'm not even sure he's awake yet."

"How long is the recovery?" I asked, wondering if my mother might bake him cookies again.

"It all depends. The doctors think that if things continue to go smoothly, he might be home in less than two weeks," my mother said.

"Okay," I said. "I'll try you tonight after you've had a chance to visit with him."

"Actually" — my mother cleared her throat — "I have plans."

It wasn't often that Malabar was alone and available in Boston, an easy drive from Plymouth, so Ben had made an excuse to be in the city, and he and my mother had a date. I could tell from her voice that she regretted the decision, that it had been a miscalculation on her part, but I also knew that she would never cancel on Ben. Malabar would slap on a dress and a smile and suppress any problematic emotions.

That lonely feeling comes from not feeling known.

"I'll keep you updated, sweetie," my mother promised.

—

On October 20, just a few days after his surgery, Charles suffered a massive stroke and died alone in his hospital room. My mother was with Ben at the time.

I arrived in Boston the next day and found Malabar weeping harder than I thought possible. It was as if a lifetime's worth of emotional chutes and trapdoors installed for self-protection decades ago had malfunctioned in a spectacular way. She couldn't avoid her feelings of sorrow and guilt. My mother's despair over Charles was beyond anything I could have imagined. Even though his death was the eventuality she had been waiting for, a prerequisite for the better life she imagined she'd have with Ben, the immensity of her grief took her—all of us—by surprise.

"He didn't deserve to die alone," Malabar said as we lay in her bed together. "Charles was so good to me, Rennie. And look at how I treated him. I gave him the worst of me."

It was true, I thought. She had.

PART II

Life can only be understood backwards; but it must be lived forwards.

— SØREN KIERKEGAARD

FOURTEEN

WHEN I FIRST got back to college, and less than two weeks after Charles's death, I learned that ocean salvagers had chipped a thick layer of corrosion off a bronze bell found within sight of the shore of a Wellfleet beach. Beneath the hardened gunk — two hundred and seventy years of sand and debris pressed into rock — the past resurfaced to reveal an inscription that identified the wreck: THE WHYDAH GALLY 1716.

I wept that Charles hadn't lived to see the headlines, proof of a pirate ship whose fate had been the object of his wonder for years. My stepfather had been nothing but good to me. He was a gentle soul whose humor and generosity had lifted our family. I went through the winter wrapped in a heavy blanket of pain. I avoided people, slept much of each day, and ate constantly, adding a protective layer of padding.

I realized I'd made a mistake that long-ago summer by signing on with my mother with such fierce purpose. I'd not felt so much as a pinprick of foreboding or dark premonition about what lay beyond the curve of time. Now that Charles was gone, I couldn't stop thinking about him, how kind he'd been and how I hadn't deserved that kindness. I began to understand that I'd crashed into something when I agreed to help my mother in her affair. I was grounded on shoals invisible from the surface and perpetually exhausted from taking on water.

—

My mother was also consumed with guilt and regret. During our phone calls, she cried and cried, blaming herself for being impatient and short-tempered with Charles during his final years, for her betrayal. What's more, his death had not granted her the life with Ben she longed for. As long as Lily was alive, my mother would be in second place; she'd be the other woman. And although she'd always have an annual income from Charles's trust, she worried constantly about money and her future.

Then about a year later, regret left as suddenly as it arrived, and the old Malabar was back.

That my mother's career was thriving certainly must have helped. In 1986, Malabar's first cookbook composed of original recipes, *Do-Ahead Dining*, was published and dedicated to Charles. My copy was inscribed *For my sweetest, dearest guinea pig/aide/therapist and friend*. The subsequent book, *Do-Ahead Entertaining*, published one year later, appeared to be dedicated to her parents, Peter, and me. But it was a ruse. My mother's father and Ben happened to share initials, albeit differently ordered, which enabled Malabar, by using initials instead of names, to dedicate the book to Ben. A misprint, she could say. A typo.

However unlikely it sounds, the friendship my mother had cultivated with Ben and Lily as a couple while Charles was alive continued following his death. The mechanics of how this threesome worked elude me to this day, but Ben and Lily helped my mother cope with the loneliness of widowhood, and she, in turn, must have provided something essential to them, even if it was only distracting them from their strained marriage. They visited each other regularly and took the occasional trip together. Ben and my mother still

saw each other on the sly, meeting in New York at the InterContinental. Whenever possible, I joined them for a power pack in their
room or at the hotel bar.

Then, during my junior year of college, my mother got the idea
that she would bring the two families together, kids and all. Determined to orchestrate a joint family getaway, Malabar found a large
house on Harbour Island in the Bahamas that was available for two
full weeks that included Christmas and New Year's. According to
her, the Southers loved the plan; they hoped that an all-expenses-
paid trip to a tropical island would entice their two children, Jack
and Hannah, both in their early thirties, to spend the holiday with
them. It did. My mother invited our extended family and even encouraged Peter and me to bring our significant others. In my case,
this was Hank from the clam bar; he'd been my boyfriend since August, when I encouraged him to extricate himself from his relationship with Sally. Malabar planned to show Ben Souther exactly what
she could pull off with a family vacation. She figured she'd string
together so many memories — exotic meals and ocean adventures
— that the Southers would talk about their trip to Harbour Island
for years to come.

I met Jack Souther in the Miami International Airport, where the
first tranche of our vacation crew — flying in from Boston, New
York, and San Diego — had arranged to converge for a meal in the
terminal. The rest of our group would arrive in dribs and drabs over
the coming week, but for forty-eight hours, it would be just five of
us: Malabar, Ben, Lily, Jack, and me. Jack had full lips, a shag of light
brown hair, and an athletic build, the result, I would come to learn,
of a rigorous daily regimen of sit-ups, pushups, and squats. The way
he stood, relaxed with his arms crossed, exuded confidence and con-
veyed a certain kind of easy masculinity. He was a decade older than
I was, could speak knowledgeably on a range of topics from international politics to the environment, and addressed people — his fa-

ther included—as "pal" or "pally," which sounded either affectionate or condescending, depending on the circumstance. Over dinner at the airport bar, I noticed Jack eyeing my shrimp cocktail. "Here, have one," I said. I dunked a large shrimp into horseradish sauce and placed it directly into his mouth, surprising us both.

The next morning, we flew to Nassau, and from there, we were taken across a clear blue ocean by a water taxi and deposited on a dock near a town dotted with pastel-colored homes and boutique hotels. After some quick wharf-side negotiations with the locals, we procured a golf cart that we loaded up with luggage and drove to the large yellow house that would be our home for the next two weeks.

Once we'd all unpacked our suitcases, Ben and Jack took off on a snorkeling adventure and Lily meandered into town in search of a good book on the island's history. My mother and I organized the kitchen, no small feat as Malabar had planned two weeks' worth of dinners. She had brought an enormous Styrofoam cooler full of frozen meat and had shipped a case of wine and a box of culinary necessities like basmati rice, Italian pasta, spices, and extra virgin olive oil. And she never traveled without her own pepper grinder.

After everything was put away, my mother suggested that we unwind and catch up out on the veranda, where fuchsia climbed the latticework and bell-shaped yellow elder shrubs released a pungent perfume. She excused herself to change while I brought out two glasses of iced tea. When my mother emerged, she was wearing a chic sun hat, oversize sunglasses, and a boldly patterned bikini beneath a sheer shift. She stretched out on the chaise longue, knee bent just so, looking as though she were posing for an advertisement for this very vacation. She sighed in contentment at her surroundings. The place—both the house and the island itself—had exceeded her expectations, and now, after weeks of planning, she just needed to allow the vacation to unfold.

But I could tell that my mother wasn't fully relaxed. She fingered the fringe of her cover-up, smoothing it over her thighs again and again. There was a lot to orchestrate here — all these people and meals — and I understood that the stakes were high. Malabar wanted to show everyone a good time, but Ben in particular; she hoped to provide him with a vision of how harmonious and fun she could make his family life — if she was at his side, his children would clamor to come on every vacation. But for that to happen, she would need to make a good impression on them now. I knew she was especially curious about Jack, the mysterious son who'd moved far away from home and who rarely returned. Ben's daughter, Hannah, would be arriving in another couple of days, but my mother was less interested in her. Men were Malabar's focus.

Attuned to her mood, I asked my mother what she thought about Jack, knowing that her first impressions of people were rarely favorable.

"I haven't made up my mind about him yet," she admitted, giving me a smile. "I certainly don't like all that 'pally' business, but I plan to give him a chance. And you?" she asked.

I returned her smile. "Well, he's a little cocky, for sure, but what's not to like? He's smart, funny, and good-looking . . . like his father." I added the part about Ben for my mother's benefit. Jack and his father did not, in fact, resemble each other, although they did share a certain rugged handsomeness.

"In any event, let's just make sure Jack has a great time on this vacation," my mother said.

A tail flickered in my peripheral vision and I turned to see an island gecko frozen on the exterior of the house. The lizard was so still that it didn't look real until the thin shutters of its eyelids lowered and opened.

My mother noticed it too and groaned. "The island's roaches."

"They're kind of cute," I said.

"I guess, if you don't mind cold-blooded." Malabar glanced over her shoulder at the gate to the courtyard to make sure that no one was within earshot. "You know that they're adopted, right? Both Jack and Hannah," she said in a whisper, as if the subject were taboo.

Did I know this? I wasn't sure I did.

"The problem was with Lily," my mother said. "Of course, everyone assumed it was Ben's issue." She paused. "Such a horrible stigma for any man to endure."

I knew then that, from Malabar's perspective, the inability to produce a son for Ben Souther—whose own father-to-son lineage stretched like a paper-doll chain umpteen generations back to the decks of the *Mayflower*—was yet another example of Lily's failings as a wife.

"What do you mean? Why did everyone think it was him?" I asked.

My mother looked baffled, as if the answer were so clear that she hardly understood my need to ask the question. "Come on, Rennie. Isn't it obvious? People assumed a man with Ben's bloodline would leave the marriage if his wife couldn't bear him children. I mean, he is a direct descendant. You and I might think that it's silly, but some people take that *Mayflower* stuff very seriously."

She went on to point out how gracious it was that Ben had never outed his wife to correct this misperception, with its unseemly assault on his masculinity.

I was listening and not listening at the same time, basking dreamily in the sensory pleasures of the island. Two days ago, I'd been in cold gray New York City, cramming for exams. Now here I was, enveloped by warmth and color. Yellow and red hibiscus sprang from large pots scattered about the lanai. In the distance, I heard the muffled voices of families returning from the beach, the bell of a bicycle, songbirds. Overhead, palm fronds rustled, and fragrant smells, absurd in their sweetness, wafted on the breeze.

I became aware that, from behind her dark glasses, my mother was watching me.

"What I wouldn't give to produce a proper heir for that man," she said.

Even without being able to see her eyes, I knew the look she wore —Malabar had an idea percolating.

"Well, I suppose *that* is something you might be able to help with," she ventured.

I pretended to whack her on the arm. "Seriously, Mom? Gross."

My mother laughed. "What? You could be our surrogate, Rennie."

I allowed myself to join in with her laughter, timidly at first and then a little louder, glad that we both understood this as a joke. "What would that make me? Mother to my baby brother or sister? Eww. That's beyond creepy."

"You're right, it is," she said.

I considered the proposal, though, and thought about what my mother was saying. Did she really want to have a child with Ben? Malabar was in her mid-fifties now, well past her fertility prime, and Ben was fourteen years her senior. No; it was impossible.

A long moment passed.

"I suppose Ben and I could make do with a grandchild," my mother conceded.

I leaned back and shut my eyes. The afternoon sun beckoned dormant freckles, and beads of water slid down our tall iced-tea glasses. My mother continued to gossip about the Southers and I listened without much interest, wishing I'd accompanied Ben and Jack on their dive. Adopted or not, Jack resembled his father constitutionally. He was self-assured, athletic, interested in all aspects of the world he inhabited, and he had a voracious appetite for action. There was something about him.

"They're not close, you know," my mother said of Ben and Jack. "It pains Ben so. I'm sure he envies the relationship you and I have."

I wondered if something in particular had come between them or if their estrangement was simply a gradual drifting apart, the natural outcome of separate lives on opposite coasts. After graduating from college in Colorado, Jack had moved to San Diego, where he'd been living ever since. He now worked full-time as a lieutenant in the city's large lifeguard department; his trips to the family home in Plymouth were rare.

My mother speculated that the rift had to do with Lily's lack of natural maternal ability. As evidence, she told me about Lily's collection of parenting books, still prominently displayed on a shelf in their library. "Honestly, Rennie, if you need a book to teach you how to be a good mother," Malabar said with disdain, "you're probably not up for the job."

On cue, the front gate squeaked and Lily pushed through. She'd been to town and had returned with a papaya, a long-flapped canvas hat to protect the back of her neck from the sun, and a thin book on the island's history and many attractions.

"Malabar," she said, holding up the book, "conch recipes!" Her voice, which had been in steady decline since I'd known her, was now set at a hoarse whisper.

"Another book, Lily?" my mother teased. "Really? You need to explore this island, not read about it."

Lily shrugged. If she was offended, she didn't show it. She never let Malabar get under her skin. She pulled a lounge chair into a shady spot, donned her unattractive hat, opened the book, and lay alongside my mother, Melanie Wilkes to her Scarlett O'Hara.

—

Ben and Jack had been tasked with finding live conches on the sandy ocean floor around the island's coral reefs during their snorkeling expedition. My mother's culinary goal for her stay on Harbour Island was to make the perfect conch fritter. The men did not disappoint, returning with two large beauties whose glossy orange-pink interiors were protected by tightly clamped brown doors. The burning question became how to coax the large snails from their shells.

Although Jack had had experience with abalone, and my mother and Ben had handled all sorts of East Coast mollusks, no one in our small group had ever tackled conch.

Lily suggested that her book might have the answer.

"Oh, Lily, but where would be the fun in that?" my mother asked.

We had moved inside. Malabar poured final splashes of rum into goblets already full of rum punch, then garnished each drink with a wedge of fresh pineapple. She wore a brightly colored island kaftan with a plunging neckline.

Lily lifted her glass and toasted. "Skoal."

We all joined in — "Skoal" — our glasses clinking merrily against one another's.

The sweet drinks slid down our throats with an icy burn. A few sips in, my mother and Ben flung themselves into one of their riotous mock fights. "What these fellas need is some heat," my mother declared, holding up one of the conches. "A brief dip in a steam bath should do the trick. It will relax their muscles and they'll release their hatches. Then we'll be able to slide their innards out."

"Wrong," Ben said. "Cold is what is called for. Ice. At least fifteen minutes in the freezer." He tapped his index finger on my mother's sternum. "Then I'll be able to slip a knife behind the operculum and pry them out."

"Impressive vocab, Dad," Jack said, chiming in from the living room. "I suggest a sledgehammer."

Game on.

I no longer remember which method won the day, but by the time we'd finished our second rum cocktails, the slick tenants had been successfully evicted and Malabar had created yet another memorable moment.

In short order, soused and bearing knives, Jack and I formed an assembly line, chopping conch meat, onions, garlic, and parsley to Malabar's precise specifications. She seasoned our mix with cay-

enne, salt, and pepper, then folded the meat concoction into a batter
of flour, eggs, and milk. When the oil was hot enough, she lowered
in rounded tablespoons of batter, which bobbed and spat furiously.
She nudged them around with a wooden spoon, turning them over
until they were an even golden brown. We ate the fritters piping hot
with a spicy lime-mayonnaise dipping sauce.

Ben, Lily, and I were used to the Malabar Show, but I could tell
that Jack was impressed. And why wouldn't he be? He'd just been
served sublime appetizers made from creatures plucked from the
ocean's floor hours earlier. Our drinks had been blended with fresh
pineapple and lime juice. My mother had even made potato chips.

It occurs to me now that Jack might have noticed the chemistry between my mother and his father that very night had we not
become engaged in a serious flirtation of our own. Ripping a page
from Malabar's book, I wore a turquoise-batik bandeau top and
matching sarong, not my typical cutoffs and T-shirt. I wasn't so
much competing with my mother as racing alongside her; I wanted
to have some of the fun that she always seemed to be having. Ditzy
with rum, I felt Jack's eyes scan my bare midriff and, with his gaze,
the tug of some invisible current.

Jack's voice was sonorous and low, in every way the opposite
of his mother's little scratch. As the evening wore on, Jack became
aware of his mother's frailty. He witnessed her several times having to tug at Ben's arm to get his attention, and he seemed struck
by the change in their dynamic. His father had been hard of hearing
for as long as Jack could remember, likely the result of Ben's love
of hunting and consequent lifetime exposure to the concussive energy of gunshots near his ears. Jack hadn't been home in a couple
of years, so he hadn't observed the progressive toll that these failing
body systems—Lily's voice, Ben's hearing—were taking on his
parents' ability to communicate.

"Exactly how does this work for you two?" Jack asked.

We had moved on to wine and were now assembled on sofas and
chairs in the living room. Malabar was in the kitchen, separated only

by a counter, preparing dinner. The pungent fragrance of Cajun spices and sautéed garlic had started to infuse the room.

"It's not a big problem," Ben assured him.

"How's that?" Jack asked.

"Well, for one thing, I took a lip-reading class," Ben said.

"Seriously?" Jack asked.

"He actually did," Lily said, though she rolled her eyes. "Your father took a single lip-reading class and when the instructor told him he had natural talent, he understood that to mean he didn't have to come back."

Jack shook his head and laughed, a chuckle tinged with cynicism. "Pally, you know you can't lip-read, right?" he said to his father. "You've missed nearly everything Mom's said tonight."

The room got strangely congested, quiet.

My mother lifted her cocktail napkin and seemed to wipe the smile off her face. She was pulsating with displeasure at Jack's interference. I could not lip-read either but I could practically see her thought bubble: *Ben hears* me *just fine*.

In an effort to lighten what was becoming a tense moment, I proposed an on-the-spot lip-reading test.

"You're on," Ben responded gamely. "I told you she was a peach," he said to Jack.

I blushed and looked at Jack.

"You were right about that," Jack replied and winked at me, causing that inner current to pull again, every molecule in my body shifting toward him.

Ben and I rearranged our chairs to face each other while the rest of the group assembled behind him so that they, too, could read my lips.

"Ready?" I asked.

Ben nodded.

How. Are. You? I mouthed with prominent exaggeration.

Jack, Lily, and my mother nodded in unison, indicating they understood my simple sentence.

Ben, however, looked momentarily confused.

Then he grinned wolfishly. "You *want* me?"

After dinner, I asked if anyone wanted to go on a constitutional. The question was reflexive at this point in my life; there was never a meal with the Southers that didn't end with my proposing a walk. Tonight, relaxed and a little drunk, I found myself eager to take one, which wasn't always the case. I wanted to go to the beach and listen to the waves.

"I'm in," Jack said.

My mother and I looked at each other with surprise. We didn't have a contingency plan for interlopers. No one had ever wanted to tag along.

"You kids have fun," Ben said. "Us old fogies will go to bed."

As soon as we went through the gate, I took Jack's hand and led him across the island to the ocean-side beach, where a warm breeze, a sky full of stars, and the mesmerizing sound of waves lapping against the shore conspired to create the perfect mood.

My boyfriend, Hank, did not enter my mind as I took this walk with Jack. No, the only thing I was able to focus on was how right everything felt—the warm night, Jack's hand wrapped around mine, soft sand underfoot. The necklace of torches strung along the curve of the beach. That tingly feeling of anticipation, constellated desire. It was as if I'd been waiting for this exact moment with this exact man.

Was this what people meant when they spoke of fate and destiny? When they described the feeling of some omniscient being operating all the puppet strings and orchestrating everything? No, I thought, and I quieted the voice in my head that suggested that this situation was not of my own making. Sure, it was a coincidence to be falling for Ben's son, but so what?

Then I kissed Jack and pushed him onto the sand.

—

It is impossible for me to revisit this thirty-year-old beach scene without questioning my motives. I do not doubt my attraction to Jack, who was magnetic and smart. But for the balance of my romantic life, I'd never once been the one to make the first move. I'd always responded to suggestion, however subtle—a look, a flirt, a touch—before pursuing a man. But with Jack it was different. From the moment I saw him in the airport, from the moment our hands touched in greeting, I felt myself careering toward him. Jack welcomed my exuberance and reciprocated quickly, but I was the initiator, not him. I fired the first shot across the bow at the airport bar when I put the shrimp into his mouth and felt his lips on my fingertips. Jack didn't happen to me; I happened to Jack.

—

Jack and I would have just two short days together before Hank arrived, and we wasted no time. In a mere forty-eight hours, Jack and I poured the foundation of our relationship, unaware of how an architectural miscalculation in the basement would go on to affect every floor in the years to come. We took runs in the morning, explored the island's coral reefs by day, and lay on the beach at night, canopied by stars. We added a new dimension to our parents' love triangle, enmeshing our families further. And although I'm sure I would have insisted otherwise at the time, I knew this was exactly what Malabar wanted.

As the rest of our group arrived in Harbour Island—my stepgrandmother, Julia; Charles's sister and niece; Hannah; Peter and Peter's girlfriend; and Hank, of course—I came to understand that Malabar was right about yet one more thing: clandestine love was electrifying. Sneaking around upped the pleasure quotient. I'd find myself restrained against a wall one moment, Jack's warm breath on my neck, his body pressed against mine. Then, at the sound of footsteps — that sweet chance of getting caught — we'd let go of each other, turn in opposite directions, and casually rejoin the group as nonchalantly as if we'd merely been getting something, lip balm or a novel, in our rooms, confident that no one had noticed our absence. We'd sneak touches at every opportunity — knees pressing under the table, fingers caressing in the passing of plates. Like our parents before us, we spoke in a language rich in innuendo. All of it thrilling. Not only was I deceiving Hank, I was outmaneuvering my mother. Truly, I believed I'd out-Malabared Malabar.

Once again, I was wrong.

FIFTEEN

AFTER THE VACATION in the Bahamas, I jettisoned Hank, and Jack and I became a couple. We decided to keep our relationship a secret; neither of us wanted to involve our parents until we were surer of how we felt about it ourselves. But that wasn't the only secret I was keeping. I hadn't told my new boyfriend that our parents were in love and had been having an affair for years. It hadn't even occurred to me to tell him.

I was a junior in college and still had a year and a half of school remaining, so Jack and I long-distanced; I took furtive trips to San Diego and he flew to New York City. On Jack's second visit to Manhattan, we spent the weekend at my father's West Village apartment while he was out of town doing research for a story.

With Malabar as my role model growing up, perhaps it is not surprising that I'd given a great deal of thought to the first home-cooked meal that I would make for Jack. It would be linguine con vongole, an easy dish rich with flavors that I knew was one of his favorites. Its success depended on the freshness of the ingredients, the quality of the olive oil, and not overcooking the clams. But I also had an ace in the hole, an idea for how to make the meal special.

In the kitchen, Jack opened a bottle of wine, poured two glasses, and sat on a stool, expecting me to begin to chop the garlic and parsley that were already on the counter. Instead, I pulled out an enormous cutting board and dumped onto it a mountain of flour. With two fingers, I created a well in the dome and into that hollow dropped three eggs and a tablespoonful of olive oil. I used my fingers to blend the mixture until what started as shaggy and sticky gathered into an uneven lump.

Jack watched, lighting up when he realized what I had in mind. "Wait," he said. "We're making the pasta?"

"Of course," I said nonchalantly. "Come on. This isn't a spectator sport."

I divided the mass into two even chunks and placed them in tandem on the board. Jack picked one up, took a quick sniff, and then squeezed it as if it were Play-Doh until it oozed between his fingers.

"Not like that," I said, and I put my hands over his and showed him how to knead properly: press down on the dough with the heel of the palm, fold the flattened mass, turn it, and press again. I took my place beside him and we massaged the dough, shoulder to shoulder in the galley kitchen, until it became pliant.

When he was done, he wrapped his arms around me and kissed my neck.

"Not so fast," I said, retrieving an old-style hand-cranked pasta machine and clamping it to the counter. "There's still work to do." I positioned Jack at the machine's arm and told him to crank as I fed the first ball through the stainless-steel rollers. We fumbled a bit initially but then got into a rhythm, turning the knob one notch tighter after every two passes, which brought the rollers a millimeter closer together. In a matter of minutes, the dough was transformed into pasta, becoming long and thin, glossy and supple. When the sheet was about five feet long, I wrangled it through the cutting rollers with Jack at the other end to catch the snaking ribbons of linguine as they emerged. When they were gathered in his arms like drapery, we walked around the dining room and laid the pasta out to dry, a few strands at a time, over the backs of chairs, across the metal arm of a standing lamp, flat on the dining-room table. After we repeated the process with the second ball of dough, my father's dining room looked like a set for a romantic comedy.

Covered in flour, giddy with wine, Jack led me into the bedroom, away from the mess of drying pasta. We were in there for a while, glad to be together after another long separation. Jack started to say something but stopped midway. He moved on top of me, propped himself up on his elbows directly over me, and tried to speak again. His eyes filled.

"What?" I said, reaching up to touch his face.

"I'm in love with you is what," he said, and his tears overflowed and spilled into my eyes.

—

It didn't take long for our parents to figure things out. After Jack disclosed to a family friend that he was seeing someone in New York, Ben put two and two together. The news spread quickly to Malabar, who was utterly unsurprised and could not have been more delighted. From her perspective, it was as if our having fallen in love confirmed the deep rightness of her love for Ben. From mine, I was just happy that Jack and I'd managed to keep our romance under wraps for the few months that we did. Falling in love with Jack without Malabar knowing allowed me to believe that I was steering the ship and somehow reassured me that my mother's being pleased had nothing to do with my trying to please her.

I was twenty-one years old, old enough to feather my nest as I wished. So why was I trying to simulate my mother's desired roost? This was not, of course, a question I asked myself at the time. After all, Jack was so self-assured and steady. There was nothing strange about a young woman falling in love with her mother's lover's son;

it was normal to prioritize your mother's secret over your boy-friend's trust. I told myself this lie so often, I believed it completely.

—

I moved to San Diego to live with Jack just weeks after receiving my BA from Columbia. I had done well in college, graduating with honors as I had in high school, but my real learning years, it would turn out, were ahead of me.

I had yet to become a person who devoured books, reflected deeply, or considered the kind of life I wanted to lead. I was a hard worker and capable, but I had chosen the path of least resis-tance to my diploma, opting for a multidisciplinary major, Urban Studies — a mix of political science, history, sociology, and anthro-pology — that allowed me to build on credits already accumulated and didn't require much academic rigor. My decision to move to San Diego was made in the same way. I had no plan. I chose California because I'd fallen in love with Jack. No part of me stopped to won-der: *Why Jack? Why San Diego?* I still believed that no decision was irrevocable.

I arrived in Pacific Beach with a large duffle bag and my elderly cat, a long-haired calico with an extra toe on each front paw. Like most cats, she was affectionate and aloof by turns. Jack's condo was a tidy rectangle of a bachelor pad decorated in unassuming neutral tones — light wood tables, an off-white sofa and chairs, beige wall-to-wall carpeting. The sofa faced an enormous television. Upstairs were two bedroom suites, a master and guest, both of which fea-tured walls of mirrored sliding doors that concealed ample closet space. Downstairs was a living/dining area, a kitchen, a half bath, and a back room with a StairMaster and a huge barbell with weights that was part gym and part office.

I hadn't been in my new home for thirty minutes when my cat hacked up a mustard-brown hairball on the light carpet. Jack's ex-hale was loud and long and rumbled with apprehension. This was not surprising. Jack was not a cat person and had agreed to let me bring mine only grudgingly. He hadn't had a pet since he'd left home to attend college fifteen years earlier. He had grown up with dogs. Throughout Jack's childhood in Plymouth, his family had had one retriever and one setter: Tor and Tap.

I had met Tor and Tap on several occasions and assumed Jack had misspoken, accidentally using the current dogs' names instead of his childhood dogs' names. But no, the mistake was mine. Jack explained that every Souther retriever was named Tor and at least two Souther setters were named Tap.

"That's . . . weird," I said. "And kind of awful."

"There have been many Tors and Taps," Jack said, exaggerating, amused by my horror. "There might have even been a set or two before Hannah and I arrived on the scene."

"I don't understand. Why not give the dogs their own names?"

Jack shrugged. He'd never thought about it.

"Seriously," I said. "Why?"

"Don't know," Jack said. "Tor and Tap were first and foremost my dad's hunting dogs." Jack explained his father's theory about one-syllable names for animals. "He says dogs understand them better."

We'd had two small terriers at 100 Essex when I was growing up. "Yap hounds," my father said with disdain when they charged his car, barking at his ankles.

"In my dad's opinion, dogs needed to be skilled and obedient," Jack continued. "The Tors and Taps were work animals. They stayed outside and slept in the garage."

"Even now?" Surely age had softened Ben's stance on this. "Even in the winter?"

Jack nodded. "You know my dad."

I wondered if I did.

My first real job was as a legislative aide to a locally elected official in which my purported area of expertise was land use and the environment. As I moved up the political career ladder in San Diego, my father began building a life there too. Around the same time I fell in love with Jack, Paul Brodeur had fallen in love with a woman from La Jolla named Margot. Aside from a brief rebound marriage to my first stepmother, my charming father had been a bachelor for twenty years with a steady string of interesting and attractive girlfriends. That he was settling down now surprised me. At first glance, Margot seemed lovely but unremarkable, a sprightly and bespectacled blonde about a decade his junior. But beneath her bookish exterior was an unconventional and sharp-witted woman, a seismologist when it came to emotional tectonics. Margot had an eye for art and small treasures, rivaled my mother in the kitchen, and owned a beautiful independent bookstore in Del Mar, a tony community known for its horseracing track.

She became a great friend to me and, over time, my confidante — an older, wise woman who was maternal in ways that Malabar was not. She asked probing questions and listened fully to my answers, a first for me.

Margot and my father threw dinner parties with their eclectic friends — writers, artists, and other intellectuals — and I never once left their home without Margot pressing a book into my hand, usually a novel. Somehow Margot divined that despite being the daughter of a *New Yorker* writer, I hadn't had a proper literary education. It was as if she knew that I had not been one of those kids who sneaked flashlights under the covers to read at night. At 100 Essex, I'd had a television within arm's reach of my bed and fell asleep every night to the ghostly sound of static.

"Books will change your life, Rennie," Margot told me, handing me a copy of *A Room of One's Own*. (I would later learn that Virginia Woolf held a special place in Margot's heart; she owned a notable collection of the author's first editions as well as other scholarly materials.) "You have no idea how much you can learn about yourself by plunging into someone else's life," Margot said.

I smiled at her, not fully understanding what she was saying but feeling a small *ping* of comprehension, an olive pit smacking the wall of my consciousness.

"You can read your way into a whole new narrative for yourself," Margot promised.

―

During one of my regular phone conversations with Kyra, with whom I had remained close since that first summer, I told my friend that I'd finally put a healthy distance between myself and Malabar.

"Three thousand miles is no small thing," I boasted.

Kyra laughed.

"What?" I said.

She stopped laughing. "Come on. You're joking."

"No. Why?"

"Never mind," she said.

"You have to tell me," I insisted.

"Look around you, Rennie. Look at who you're living with."

The cat was curled on the sofa beside Jack, who was watching the news.

Oh, that. I felt my face redden. "Don't be ridiculous," I said. "The two are completely unrelated."

My mother's romance with Ben, going strong for eight years, was the alternate reality I'd grown up in. I was so used to it that it didn't seem remotely strange to me. I'd been their sidekick and chief collaborator all along, weathering close calls, suspicious spouses, a blackmail threat. By now my mother's friends knew about the affair and my role in it, and none of them had ever questioned the propriety of my involvement. I didn't understand Kyra's fixation on the coincidence. But she wouldn't let it go; so many people knew, but Jack did not. Didn't that concern me?

It did, and it didn't. The thought roiled in my mind constantly, like a pebble caught in the ocean's swash. I let myself believe that I was protecting Jack by not telling him and found comfort in the fact that he was not particularly interested in his family. He was not in touch with his sister, with whom he felt he had nothing in common. He was not particularly close to his parents. And he definitely had no interest in finding out about his biological roots. None. Here, his lack of curiosity fascinated me. How could someone *not* want to know where he came from? I didn't understand it at all.

"Have you ever thought about whether you have biological brothers or sisters?" I asked Jack. We were taking an early-evening stroll on the boardwalk of Pacific Beach, one of Jack's favorite places. Surely he must be curious about how the genes that made him might express themselves differently in someone else.

I stared out at the long expanse of gray — the boardwalk, the drab wedge of sand, the dark ocean — and couldn't help but compare it unfavorably to Nauset Beach. I missed the dunes and plovers and the nooks of inlets where egrets balanced on one leg in the shallows. Unlike Orleans, here, color came from two sources: the city's orange lifeguard vehicles that methodically cruised the beaches and the neon swimwear of the people who shot past us on Rollerblades. It was the middle of the summer and I longed for Cape Cod. Luckily, we'd be headed east soon. My mother had recently offered Peter and me the use of the guesthouse for a full two weeks each during the summer. Malabar wanted her children home, and I planned to take full advantage of the gift, now and forever.

"Why would I want to find out about people I don't know?" Jack said.

His response was incomprehensible to me. *How could you not want to know?* I was endlessly fascinated by all the characters in my family I didn't know — my grandmother's sister who'd died from scarlet fever as a toddler; my parents' secret half siblings (each of them had one and had made the discovery at an early age; I'd met my mother's half brother, but my father's half brother, with whom he shared a name, would remain a mystery). And Christopher, of course. Always Christopher. Who might he have become had he lived, and how would that have altered all of our lives? Wasn't curiosity a simple fact of human nature?

I tried another tack. "Let's say your biological parents were young and had no choice but to give you up. Maybe your mom was sick? Wouldn't you want to know that, at least?"

"My mom did have cancer, as you know," Jack said, reminding me that he had only one mother, Lily, and she had survived Hodgkin's lymphoma. "What she went through in treatment is why she has no voice today. It's why she couldn't get pregnant." He took a breath to summon his patience. "Look, Rennie, I've turned out okay. My parents and I might not be close the way you are with your mom, but I have no complaints. They're good parents. They do their best. Why would I want to hunt around for something that has the potential to hurt me? I don't see the point."

Jack's instinct to protect himself might have been the most alien thing I'd ever encountered. I'd never had a wound—emotional or physical—that I didn't probe repeatedly. In that very moment, I probably wondered for the thousandth time whether my mother, if given the choice, would have traded me for Christopher.

Jack was my opposite. He was measured, calm in every crisis. That's what he got paid for. He'd recently been promoted and now ran the San Diego lifeguard department, one of three emergency-services agencies in the city. In any given week, he might have to dive into dangerous surf to pull out a panicked swimmer, give orders to teams of rescuers in all manner of chaotic situations from law enforcement incidents to natural disasters, or deliver bad news to a victim's family members in a voice so soothing that it reassured even as the words devastated. I'd seen him perform CPR on a fellow diner at a restaurant and five minutes later pick up the conversation exactly where we'd left off before he'd bolted to save that person's life.

Jack was not a guy who looked for emotional drama. He had never lived with a woman before. Ours was, he let me know, the most serious relationship he'd ever entered. But once I'd settled in San Diego and we no longer had to trek epic distances to be together, I missed his outsize professions of love. Now that we were a committed couple, Jack was pulling back emotionally, eager to return to his routine. His daily habits—reading the paper, performing calisthenics, going for soft-sand beach runs—were what anchored him to himself. The man was a doer of sit-ups and pushups, a guy who, twice weekly—no matter what—shut himself in the back room and wrestled an enormous barbell, groaning and swearing in pain throughout his short anaerobic workout, emerging fifteen minutes later covered in sweat, vessels swollen and pulsating. In San Diego, Jack ate only one meal a day: dinner.

Jealous of his devotion to his routine, I tried to disrupt it, constantly and unsuccessfully attempting to entice him in other directions. I craved grand gestures from him just as my mother had from Ben and wanted to be able to ignite Jack's passion and cause him to do spontaneous things. Did he want to sleep in on Sunday morning and linger in bed for a long while? He did not. How about breakfast just this once, a bagel and cream cheese while we read the paper? Nope. Or maybe a morning hike together in lieu of his run? Jack would not budge.

But as we were strolling on the very beach where he took his daily runs, it occurred to me that Jack's inclination to avoid life's emotional potholes provided me with an opportunity. Maybe he wouldn't want to know about our parents' love affair. I decided to test my theory.

"I have something I need to tell you," I said in a tone serious enough that he stopped walking. "It's a secret. I've been keeping it for a long time."

We sat down on the sand beside each other, looking out to sea, studying the waves silently for a while. The sun was lowering over the water, a sight I'd found disorienting since moving to the West Coast. On Cape Cod, of course, the sun emerged from the ocean, and its daily morning trajectory over the Atlantic was, in fact, how I got my bearings. North was to the left. The whole world felt backward here, like I was always headed in the wrong direction.

"Does your secret have to do with us?" Jack asked. I could hear a hint of dread in his voice.

"Yes and no," I hedged. "It has to do with our parents more than us. Still, it could have repercussions. Tangentially." I let that sink in for a bit. "It's pretty big, Jack."

He stared out at the ocean, examining something I couldn't see —a rip current or undertow.

"Do you want to know?" I asked.

Jack looked at me. His blue eyes were clear with certainty. He shook his head no. "I love you, Ren. You love me. That's all that matters."

I felt awash in relief. "You sure?"

He nodded.

Jack didn't want to know.

It's worth mentioning that Jack does not recall having this conversation. Perhaps because it took place close to three decades ago, or maybe because the secret was mine and its gravity didn't register with him at the time. Why would it? Only I knew that I was talking about our parents' affair, the centerpiece of my life. For all Jack knew, I was just lobbing another overly emotional pitch his way—I had done a good deal of that during our short time together—and he did his best not to swing at those. Jack was in his early thirties and steered clear of drama; at twenty-two, I drove headlong toward it.

Either way, before I became involved with Jack, my mother's secret was, at its core, about her, and that changed when I made the first move on Jack. I set something different into motion and Malabar's secret became my secret too, even if I didn't want to admit it.

That memory aches. I wish that I'd had the courage to insist on telling Jack the truth that evening on Pacific Beach. If only I'd hauled that secret out of the darkness and shone a floodlight on it, maybe we'd have had the chance to begin our relationship authentically or, perhaps, to end things on the spot. Instead, I allowed the secret to fester and grow.

SIXTEEN

THESE WERE UNEASY years for Malabar. With Charles gone, my mother's relationship with Ben lacked its former balance. He was still married; she was widowed. He needed to conceal their love; she wanted to shout it from the rooftops. Patience was not one of her virtues. She had grown even more obsessed with Lily and her health and could see that although Ben's wife was frail, she showed no signs of looming demise. My mother begged Ben to figure something out, to find a way for them to spend more time together, but their agreement had always been that they'd wait until their spouses died to do anything permanent. That was the deal.

"I wonder what would happen if Lily actually found out and had to face facts," my mother ventured during one of our weekly phone calls.

"I'm pretty sure Lily already knows on some subconscious level," I said, unable to imagine that she did not. My mother and Ben were not exactly subtle.

I was on the downstairs phone, standing in our galley kitchen, and I could hear Jack bumping around overhead. The coast was clear.

"Oh, Lily knows, all right. I'm sure she does, deep down," my mother said. "But I'm wondering what she would do if she was forced to confront it head-on. If the whole thing was out in the open."

According to my mother, Ben had said on countless occasions that if he were forced to make a decision between Lily and her, he would choose my mother absolutely. His constant refrain: "I'd sooner die than live without you."

I leaned back against the counter. "Mom, exactly what are you proposing here?"

Jack trotted down the stairs, newspaper tucked under his arm. He smiled at me as he passed on his way to the back room where his barbell awaited. *Everything okay?* he mouthed. I nodded. Although Jack's weight workout would take at least fifteen minutes and the door was always shut, I wanted to get off the phone.

"I'm not proposing anything," she said, irritated. "I'm thinking aloud is all. I'm wondering, if Lily knew with certainty that her husband was in love with me, would it force something? Change the situation somehow?"

"Sounds dangerous," I said quietly.

"Well, Rennie, perhaps you need to consider things from Lily's perspective for a change," my mother said without a trace of irony. "For all you know, the news that he would stay with her even though he was in love with someone else might come as a huge relief to her. Maybe with Charles gone and me single, she lives in terror that Ben will up and leave her one of these days. Perhaps Lily would feel reassured if the truth were openly acknowledged. Then she could feel safe in her marriage and I could . . ."

"You could what, Mom? What would you do differently?"

"Well, for starters, I could have some more time with the man."

"I don't know about that," I said. I heard the clank of metal against metal, the barbell being lifted off its frame. "I really can't have this conversation right now."

"Okay, honey." My mother sighed. "But fair warning — some-time soon, I just might need to pull the trigger."

———

Within a year, Jack succumbed to my cat's charms. Most mornings when I padded downstairs, I would find her purring, nestled beside him on the sofa as he read the newspaper. Jack spoke to the cat as if she were human and dutifully attended to her needs — scratches be-hind the ears, kibble in a stainless-steel bowl. He would even spread a line of the fishy-smelling ointment that helped her digestion on his index finger and let her lick it off. My cat was more effective at com-ing between Jack and his routine than I was.

Already old, our cat became enfeebled the summer of 1989; she slept constantly and had a hard time keeping food down. When we brought her to the veterinarian's office for the final time, she could hardly raise her head. Jack and I each laid a hand on her soft fur as the doctor injected her with pentobarbital. She fell asleep purr-ing and died in a matter of minutes. We both sobbed on the way home, throughout that day, and for several days following. If I'd had doubts about Jack's emotional capacity, they were extinguished. Jack did much more than comfort me; his loss felt as substantial as my own.

Later that same week, while we were sitting on a slope of grassy meadow in Kate Sessions Park, leaning against each other, Jack reached into his pocket, turned, knelt before me, and presented me with an engagement ring.

"I love you, Rennie, and want to spend my life with you," he said and then choked up. I began to cry too. "Will you marry me?"

The proposal did not come as a complete surprise. Jack and I had looked at engagement rings together, learned about carats and clarity, and discussed styles. But none of that had seemed real. Un-til now.

Over Jack's shoulder, the view was expansive: the bay and the ocean, the downtown buildings, and the Coronado Bridge beyond. The Hotel del Coronado with its red-tiled roof looked like a fairy-tale castle in the distance.

I was twenty-three and not someone who'd fantasized much about weddings. I could not point to a single marriage I'd witnessed up close that I admired for having triumphed lastingly over life's hurdles. My parents, in their late fifties, had each been married twice and were now eyeing spouse number three. As far as I could tell, marriage did not seem to be a sustainable or ideal institution. And yet, when Jack proposed, I did not hesitate to say yes, the ring slid-ing effortlessly onto my finger.

—

I called my mother to tell her the news as soon as I got home.

"Oh, darling," she said. "That's so wonderful. I couldn't be hap-pier."

I told her that we hoped to have the wedding on Cape Cod the following July, at her home, if possible.

"Of course," she said. "We'll have it on the front lawn. Keep it simple. Nauset Bay is more splendid than any chapel." Then Mala-bar was silent for a moment. I assumed she was composing the menu in her head or imagining a dance with the groom's father. "Guess what?" she said. I heard a hitch in her breathing and waited.

"I've made a decision."

My mother liked dramatic moments, and she stretched this one out.

"What?" I asked. "What is it?"

"I'm going to give you the family necklace. I always said you would wear it on your wedding day. And now you will." Her voice cracked with emotion.

"Oh, Mom," I said, stunned. "Are you sure?"

"Positive. My gift to my girl on her wedding day. Your grand-mother would have loved that."

I'd waited my whole life for my mother to offer me the necklace. "Describe it to me again," I said. I hadn't seen it in years.

"You could actually forget?" Then Malabar recited her favorite quote about ingratitude: "'How sharper than a serpent's tooth it is to have a thankless child.'"

"Of course I remember it, Mom," I said, chagrined to have already bungled this moment. And truthfully, I could picture it, all those chunky rubies and diamonds and emeralds, each set into its own panel, each rectangle framed by dozens of delicate pear-shaped diamonds and fringed with clusters of freshwater pearls. "I just want to hear you describe it again."

Since I was a child, Malabar had always insisted that the necklace's worth was incalculable. As a teenager, I offended her by asking why she hadn't gotten it appraised.

"Because it's priceless," she'd said, her voice flat. "Un-appraisable." End of discussion.

But the stories Malabar used to tell me about the mythic piece of jewelry captured my imagination as a girl.

"A Sikh maharaja bestowed it upon his bride during a wedding spectacle," my mother would whisper, lingering over the foreignness of the word *maharaja*. "There were elephants in gold headdresses, camels festooned with intricately embroidered cloth . . ."

Her descriptions were so vivid that I almost believed she'd attended this thousand-year-old extravaganza.

On the rare occasions when she brought the necklace out, I would finger the velvet case — purple, the color of royalty — and stare at all those blinking diamonds wondering, as any little girl might, if the necklace had magical powers. I felt sure it did.

"The maharaja personally selected each gem," my mother would insist. "Imagine . . . every topaz, sapphire, and diamond handpicked from thousands."

The story would change a bit with each retelling, but never the great fortune of its recipients — that Mughal empress, rajmata, princess . . . and, someday, me.

More than anything, my mother loved telling how her father had hidden the necklace from her mother, who'd fallen in love with it on a trip to India. Apparently, my grandmother wanted it desperately, but my grandfather scoffed at her. *Don't be ridiculous, Vivian. It's far too extravagant.* But secretly, he'd bought it for her, telling the jeweler if he ever breathed a word to Memsahib — and here, my mother always paused for effect — he'd cut out the poor man's tongue.

But we all know that getting what you wish for often comes at a price. Vivian's life was upended once again by a husband who had multiple affairs and secretly fathered a child out of wedlock. When Malabar graduated from college, my grandmother gave her the necklace in an elaborate gesture. She placed the crushed-velvet box into a larger box and wrapped that box, then she put that gift-wrapped box into a larger box and wrapped that one too, going on and on until there were ten nested boxes, the final one big enough to hold a television set. As my young mother opened one box after the next, did she dare to hope about what might be inside? I imagine she did.

The old refrain from my childhood echoed in my head: *Rennie, you must promise me that you'll never, ever sell or give away this necklace, no matter what.*

My reply: *I never will.*

I'm not sure if I can trust you with it. Another refrain.

You can, I always insisted.

I should bequeath the necklace to a museum where it will be safe and appreciated.

I'll treasure it forever, I promised.

Always?

Always.

Well, then, my mother would say, *if you're very, very good, you shall wear it on your wedding day.*

I couldn't believe that it was finally happening.

SEVENTEEN

THE CALL CAME on a Sunday morning in late February, a month that saw no notable seasonal change in Southern California. The days were shorter and slightly cooler, but mostly, San Diego remained as it always was: bright, sunny, temperate. We were still in bed when Jack picked up the receiver and said hello. We'd been talking about our upcoming wedding, now five short months away.

So far, plans were proceeding smoothly. The invitations, simple and elegant, had arrived and needed only to be addressed. Jack's groomsmen were enthusiastic about the prospect of a week on Cape Cod, and my bridesmaids were all lined up: Kyra and three other close friends, one from childhood, two from college. My mother had found a caterer, my father a jazz quartet, and my aunt, a minister, had agreed to officiate. In two months, Jack and I would make a last prewedding trip to Massachusetts to sample the menu, taste the wine, select music for the official dances, and finalize everything from flowers to tablecloths to wedding cake to wedding vows.

There had been only one glitch so far: Earlier in the week, while watching the local news, we'd learned that the owners of the La

Jolla bridal boutique where I'd purchased my wedding gown had filed for bankruptcy and skipped town, leaving dozens of brides-to-be without dresses. Luckily for me, time was on my side. I was disheartened and inconvenienced, but I knew I'd be able to find another dress between now and July.

What had rattled me more than anything was the deception. Just a few weeks earlier, I'd entered the store and felt at home immediately. I'd brought along a photograph of my mother's necklace with the goal of finding a wedding gown that could do it justice. The owner of the store, a stately older woman, took her time with me. She examined the picture of the heirloom carefully and determined a portrait-style neckline would best highlight the piece.

I spent hours trying on gowns, stepping up onto a white-skirted platform surrounded by large mirrors as the woman positioned every dress just so and elaborated on its unique attributes—pearl buttons, a well-placed ruffle, intricate lacework. I could take in my reflection from every angle. Meanwhile, she fussed over me like a daughter, describing how each dress made me look—sophisticated, innocent, regal. When I stepped into an unadorned pleated silk gown, she said, "That's the one."

I saw that she was right. The dress was perfect.

"My work here is done," she said. "You're going to be spectacularly beautiful in this gown and the necklace will shine." She went on to offer me bits of marital advice while showing me shoes, veils, and other bridal accoutrements. "Best buy it all at once. You'll feel great not to have to think about any of this again."

I was grateful for her kindness and happy to pay the hefty deposit, 50 percent of the total. Of course, it had all been a charade, an elaborate scheme to rob me and, no doubt, other unsuspecting brides. The proprietor had to have known all along that she was going out of business.

"Hello," Jack said again into the receiver.

I heard the rasp of Lily's scratchy voice greet him on the other end, but she moved quickly past small talk. Jack's mother had some urgent news to impart.

"Take it easy, Mom," Jack said, trying to calm her. "I can't hear you. You need to slow down," he said gently. He looked confused. Lily had been having heart problems and I wondered if she'd gotten bad news about her health.

Then abruptly, Ben got on the line.

"What's up?" Jack asked. "Why's Mom so upset?"

I could hear Ben's voice as clearly as if he were talking on speakerphone and it took only about three words for me to realize that this was *the* conversation. It was finally happening, *this* moment. The scene that my mother and I had imagined unfolding in a thousand different ways was unraveling before me right now as I sat in bed with Ben's son.

My heart sped up. I bolted upright and looked at Jack, who was staring back at me dumbfounded, uncomprehending.

I nodded and tried to convey absolutely everything to Jack in a look, my mind careening from thought to thought: *Yes, this is the secret I was telling you about . . . I'm sorry, I should have told you myself . . . I didn't have a lot of options . . . It wasn't my fault . . . There's no road map for this . . . What are you supposed to do when you fall in love with your mother's lover's son?*

But at this moment, I heard these for what they were: excuses. Jack would now surely hate my mother for breaking up his family, and he'd blame me for keeping her secret. His mother would never forgive me for my role in the affair. This would be the end of us.

Here was Ben, revealing the secret we'd tended for a decade, but the conversation was not proceeding how my mother or I had imagined it would. Ben was apologizing profusely, yes, I could hear that, but he was not explaining to Jack the difficult road that lay ahead for their family. He was not telling his son that while he cared deeply for Jack's mother, Lily, he had fallen in love with someone else, *my* mother, Malabar. Ben was decidedly not explaining that he was leaving his marriage of forty-five years.

No, something different was happening. Ben was apologizing for the "terrible mistake" he'd made. This "betrayal," was how he put it, this "affair." The person on the other end of the line did not sound like the man I knew. Where was the self-assuredness and the swagger? Where was the confident man who knew how to do everything from dress a deer to take over a company? There was desperation in this voice. He was pleading. This was not the man who'd promised he'd always love and take care of my mother.

Where the hell was that Ben?

The man on the line wanted his wife's forgiveness. He wanted his son's forgiveness. He was begging for it. This man, this stranger on the phone, evidently had a great deal at stake.

"I'm so sorry—" the voice said.

Had Ben already called my mother? I wondered. Or was it possible that Malabar was still savoring a late-morning cup of tea along with a buttered slice of toast and fresh preserves, enjoying what would turn out to be the last moments she would ever have thinking Ben Souther would always choose her over Lily? I glanced at the clock on our bedside table. It was almost noon on the East Coast. Instantaneously, my worry had shifted from the catastrophe befalling Jack to the one raining down on my mother. I was already swimming in her grief.

"I'm so ashamed for what I've put you and your mother and your sister through," Ben continued. "I hope someday you'll be able to forgive me."

I hadn't been included in the list of aggrieved parties. If there were good guys and bad guys in this fiasco, it was clear that I was in the wrong camp, and Lily knew it. I felt nauseated and my hands started to shake.

Jack, however, remained as calm as ever. He seemed to have skipped right over shock, disbelief, and anger and landed on the terra firma of rationality.

"I understand, Dad," he said into the receiver. "Yes, I understand," he repeated. I watched his head go up and down in a barely perceptible nod. "It's understandable, it's just not acceptable."

No part of me should have been surprised at the speed with which my fiancé reconciled himself to the idea that his father had been having a decade-long love affair — never mind that the woman was his godfather's wife, his mother's friend, and, most incredibly, his soon-to-be mother-in-law.

(In the weeks and months to come, Jack would often repeat variations on the phrase *Understandable but not acceptable*. It became our mantra, a distilled morsel of truth that we could chew on as we tried to swallow a decade of deceit, my own included.)

Somehow this phone conversation was still not over. Ben had one final thing to say, a last promise to make. He swore to Jack on everything he held dear that he would never see or speak to my mother again.

Jack and I were getting married in July. Ben's promise would be impossible to keep, of course, and we all knew it. There would be other family occasions as well, perhaps grandchildren someday. Our union would ensure these two families remained enmeshed for years to come.

"I'm so, so sorry," I whispered after Jack hung up. Tears stung my eyes.

"You knew this. You knew about this," Jack said.

I nodded.

"Why didn't you tell me?" Jack asked.

"I tried," I said. "I honestly tried." It wasn't easy to explain to him what I didn't understand myself. The narrative I had convinced myself of — that I'd tried to tell Jack the truth and he'd opted not to know — suddenly seemed ludicrous. "I was only fourteen," I said, and I apologized again.

"Look, Rennie, it's not your fault," Jack said.

Oh, but it is, I thought. Perhaps some part of me had been hungering for this disaster all along. At least now Jack would finally see me for who I really was: a girl so lost she couldn't tell right from wrong or separate her own feelings from her mother's. And perhaps, if we teased apart these emotions and untangled my complicated history, we could set things straight and have a fresh start. He would know what I'd done and love me despite it, and I'd be free from the immense burden I'd been carrying.

"It's their fault," Jack insisted. "My father. Your mother. Two of the most unbelievably self-centered people I've ever known. Charles was my godfather. He was Dad's best friend. What kind of person sleeps with his best friend's wife? And think about my mother. Can you imagine what she's going through? You think you love and know someone only to find out he's been deceiving you. Honestly, the whole thing is reprehensible."

I began to weep. Wasn't that exactly what I'd done to Jack? Kept him in the dark? And I'd never once tried to imagine what Lily might feel.

"And you," said Jack, taking my face in his hands. "You were just a kid. That's the most unbearable part of it."

I stifled the urge to insist on my own complicity. I wanted to see things from Jack's perspective, one in which I was an innocent sucked into a drama not of my own making or choosing, in which I was blameless.

"How could my father possibly have gone along with involving you? And your mother. That woman is—"

"My mom was just—" I was about to explain that Malabar couldn't help falling in love.

"Stop," Jack interrupted me. "You don't even want to know what I think of Malabar."

EIGHTEEN

A FEW WEEKS LATER, Jack and I headed to Massachusetts to visit
our parents and finalize wedding plans. Since Ben had chosen to stay
with Lily, my mother was in a state of abject despair. Every one of
our conversations ended with her bewildered "How could he have
done this to me, Rennie?" But I could not attend to her broken heart
just yet. Our first stop was the Southers in Plymouth. No sooner had
I pushed through the revolving doors at Logan Airport in Boston
and gotten a whiff of brackish New England air than I experienced
Lily's anguish like a slap across the face. Even though she was still
forty miles away, her pain felt more real to me here than it had in
California. As we cruised down I-93 toward Cape Cod and the islands, it felt less like Jack was driving and more like we were being
pulled home by some invisible force.

We would spend two days with Jack's parents, the balance of the
week with my mother, and then have dinner with my father, who
lived on Cape Cod when he wasn't in San Diego with Margot. This
arrangement felt like yet another divorce, reminding me of my fail-
ure to be fair, always granting a disproportionate amount of time to
my mother.

Jack's foot was heavy on the gas pedal, and the afternoon sun pulsed through the trees along the highway, rhythmic and hypnotic, dislodging bits of a disjointed monologue I hadn't known was stored in my head.

I'm so sorry, Lily. I was only fourteen. I never meant to hurt you. I love your son, I promise I do. I am sorry. I am sorry. I am sorry.

A day or two after Jack received the call from his parents, I'd sent my mother-in-law-to-be a letter apologizing for my involvement in the affair. To apologize seemed like the proper thing to do, although the correct response in this situation was anybody's guess. I also wanted to present an official version of events from my perspective, to set the record straight. As I recall, everything I wrote in the letter was true, and yet I must have padded corners and rounded edges to accommodate the aspects of myself that needed protection: my mother's confidante, Jack's fiancée, a mixed-up young woman who desperately wanted to feel like she was still a good person.

"Everything okay?" Jack asked in the car, resting a hand on my thigh.

Everything was decidedly not okay. I didn't know how I could face Lily. Or Ben, for that matter. And I kept imagining my mother nursing her broken heart with a bottle of bourbon. My skin crawled with invisible ants, and the seat belt dug into my neck. I focused on a flock of geese flying overhead in a long V.

"Remember, this is about them, not us," he said.

I didn't know how he could believe this, though it wouldn't serve me well to press the point. It was far easier for us to fixate on their problems and not our own.

If Jack felt anger or concern that I'd kept this secret from him, he hadn't expressed it. Jack placed blame squarely on Ben and Malabar's shoulders. He was furious with our parents. I understood his rage and perspective, but I had no sense of an injustice done to me. Instead, I was guilt-ridden and made excuses for everyone's behavior, my own included.

One kiss, and Malabar had fallen hopelessly in love with Ben. *Was that so very wrong?* This was what I kept asking myself. Malabar hadn't set out to hurt anyone. She just wanted the happy ending that had been promised. And what was she to do now that the prince had gone off script? My mother's broken heart felt like my own. Lily and Ben still had each other—their life together, their home, all those exotic trips. Malabar was the one who had come up empty.

I had grown up with this drama, and even though I was starting to see the situation with adult eyes, my fealty remained with my mother, whose pain seemed to eclipse all others'. I also knew that if Jack's and my roles had been reversed, I wouldn't have been able to forgive him so readily or overlook the fundamental issue of misplaced loyalty. I'd cleaved to my mother rather than the man I'd promised to spend my life with, a fundamental—indeed biblical—betrayal.

We drove the rest of the way to Plymouth in silence.

Even as early as May, Lily's garden was something to behold. Along the Southers' driveway, cherry trees blossomed and tulips and daffodils burst forth with the promise of more to come, which, after a brutal New England winter, was no small covenant. From the bright green hill of their front lawn, a flock of white pigeons took off in synchronized flight. *Beautiful,* I thought. As if reading my mind, Jack mentioned that they might be dinner. There was a pigeon coop on the other side of the house and a bucket over which Ben would drain the pigeons' blood after slitting their necks.

I heard Ben before I saw him.

"How do!" he called, rushing out to greet us.

He and Jack back-patted briefly, and then Ben came around to my side. I felt Lily's eyes on us from somewhere, behind a curtain perhaps. I glanced up at the kitchen window, but its reflection yielded nothing. Ben hugged me tightly and didn't let go.

"I'm so sorry, honey," he whispered into my ear, and I felt his shoulders heave against mine. His cheeks were smooth and smelled of shaving cream. "I love you so much, and I hope someday you'll forgive me. You'll never know how I regret my actions."

So here was my apology at last, but what did *sorry* mean in this context? Did Ben regret that he'd involved me as a child without thinking through the ramifications? Was he sorry for the pain he was causing his son and, by extension, me? Or was he talking to my mother, sending her a private message that I was supposed to deliver? Or, another possibility, was he sorry for colossally miscalculating what his wife's reaction would be? For that is how Lily found out, I learned. In the end, Ben had simply decided to tell her.

He'd reasoned that his wife's depression wasn't about her failing heart but due to some intuition about the situation with Malabar, heightened since Charles had died. Ben thought he could relieve Lily's anxiety and assuage her fears by assuring her that although, yes, he was in love with my mother, he had no plans to leave his marriage. I recalled my phone conversation with my mother on this topic. How wrong she had been about the potential outcome.

Where was Lily? I wondered. Her eyes were all over this reunion, I knew. I could feel her presence but could not see her face.

Ben led us past the main house to a small guest cottage with a wraparound covered porch. He told us to freshen up and join them when we were ready for a drink, and then he left. We'd never stayed in the guesthouse as a couple before, though Jack spent summers there during his college years. Was I exiled from the main house? The single room was perhaps twenty square feet and might have felt cozy were it not for the mounted heads, antlers, and horns that covered every inch of the walls.

"Mom gives Dad a ten-trophy limit in the house," Jack said. "The rest go here."

I unpacked, kicked off my shoes, and stretched out on the sofa bed, which had been turned down. When I looked up, I found myself staring into the nostrils of an elk whose giant chin extended out over the pillows. Not so many years ago, I'd helped my mother grind the meat of an elk Ben had killed, dropping raw chunks of it into the top of her old-fashioned crank, which extruded them out the side in spaghetti-like strands. She used the meat to make a lasagna, adding extra ricotta to mitigate the gaminess. Now it occurred to me that the wild-game cookbook, our ruse to give Ben and Malabar time together, might never see the light of day. Jack lay down on his side, facing me.

"Am I crazy or did you once tell me that your father smooshed a bloody duck into your face?" I asked, vaguely recalling a disturbing story Jack had recounted when we were first dating.

"Affirmative," Jack said.

Unlike his father, Jack had never been much of a hunter or fisherman. He didn't like the cold and didn't have the patience those activities required. Nonetheless, when Jack was a kid, Ben would once in a while succeed in cajoling him into a predawn duck hunt with Tor and Tap. On one of these outings, when Jack was around ten, he finally managed to shoot a duck. His father was overjoyed at Jack's first kill and whooped and hollered when Tor retrieved the bird and dropped it at his feet. Ben picked up the duck, spread its feathers apart to reveal the wound, and excitedly beckoned Jack over. When Jack bent down for a closer look, Ben grabbed his son by the scruff of the neck and ground the bird's bloody backside into his face, part of some hunting rite of passage.

I rolled onto my side so that Jack and I faced each other. Jack was not adept in the language of emotion, but his expression was full of love. "Ready?" he asked.

Who could ever be ready for this, I wondered.

"Ready," I answered.

When we walked into the kitchen, everything looked more or less as it always had, and yet there was a disturbing quiet in the room.

We were on high alert, our ears up and our noses twitching like rabbits'. There was Lily, leaning against the countertop. She was as thin and brittle as I'd ever seen her, but there was a new fierceness about her too. Her wiry arms were crossed. This was *her* kitchen, *her* home, *her* family. I was on her turf now and there were new rules. When she saw Jack, her face softened and she smiled, opening her arms. Jack walked past me to embrace his mother as Lily regarded me over his shoulder. It was not an unkind look, but it made me understand that Jack had been hers before he was mine and that she'd been waiting for me, for this encounter. It would be, perhaps, the closest she'd ever get to confronting her adversary, perhaps her only opportunity to say her piece.

In this moment, it was as if a new circuit in my brain's fuse box had been flipped, suddenly illuminating Lily as a whole person. Until then I'd seen her only through Malabar's eyes: an ordinary woman who was holding back an extraordinary man, keeping him from the life he should have been living. Growing up, I had viewed Lily as the character created by my mother, bookish, plain, practical to the point of boring. But she was before me now, looking as formidable as hell. Here was a woman who'd survived Hodgkin's lymphoma, infertility, and now infidelity. I had been wrong on Harbour Island; Lily was not the Melanie Wilkes in this story. She was Scarlett O'Hara. And she wasn't going down without a fight.

When Lily's husband of forty-five years had explained to her that he'd been carrying on an affair with my mother—a woman she considered a friend—and wished to continue doing so, Lily disabused him of that notion at warp speed, jerking his chain so violently that he heeled immediately. Ben had grown up in this town of Plymouth, Massachusetts, where he was a pillar of the community, a successful businessman, a prominent *Mayflower* descendant, and a family man. Was he prepared to give all that up and have his good name dragged through the mud?

As it turned out, he was not.

I was still not quite sure how much Lily knew about my involvement. Had Ben told her everything? How often had Lily replayed moments from the past? Me at fourteen initiating the clamming expedition the day after that first kiss; me at fifteen grabbing their hands and tugging them out the door for countless evening walks; me at sixteen participating in their wild-game cookbook; me at seventeen, eighteen, nineteen, twenty, artfully and fully engaged in this affair. Had Lily tabulated all those after-dinner constitutionals? Had she been told that I used to meet him and Malabar at the InterContinental for drinks while I was in college? Had she identified me as the mastermind behind the false-letter-writing campaign?

And now I was about to marry her son. Lily knew that I loved Jack—I was sure of this—but she also understood the depth of my mother's influence and, no doubt, could see things still invisible to me.

My heart was beating so fast it felt as if one of Ben's pigeons were nailed to my chest.

"Who needs a drink?" my future father-in-law asked.

We all did.

The beverages were poured, consumed, and replenished, tequila for Lily, beer for Jack, red wine for me. Ben made himself a gin and tonic, something I'd never seen him drink before but that turned out to be his favorite cocktail. Why had he never had it with my mother? Because Malabar detested gin.

Dinner was Jack's favorite, the New England classic of steamed lobsters and corn. To that end, an enormous pot filled with a few inches of boiling water rattled its lid on the stove. Ben grabbed four large lobsters out of the sink, two in each of his enormous hands. Lily lifted the lid, and in they went. Ben slapped down the top with a bang and held it in place as the lobsters thrashed for a minute before the steam quieted them permanently. Meanwhile, Lily removed a piping-hot cast-iron skillet from the oven and set it on the stovetop. She put in a dollop of oil and a measured teaspoon of salt, then poured in her special cornbread batter, which met the pan with a hiss. This recipe, passed down through Lily's family, had found its way into one of my mother's Do-Ahead Dining columns.

We sat down at the small rectangular table in the kitchen. Ben took his usual place at the head, and Jack sat opposite him on a built-in leather bench seat under the window. This left Lily and me to face each other across the shortest gulf, an expanse of a couple of feet; she was close enough to reach across the table and hit me if she wished.

Ben arranged the lobsters on oval platters and placed an ear of corn between each one's claws, just like at a restaurant. As he dispensed tools to excavate the meat—nutcrackers, kitchen shears, cocktail forks, and a single large butcher knife—he launched into a rambling apology where he acknowledged his guilt and expressed regret for hurting Lily and putting us all in a difficult situation. But his remorse came across as broad and obligatory—more performed than felt—and when the monologue petered out, we were left staring awkwardly at our plates.

The silence was broken when Lily cracked the long tail section of her lobster, causing a projectile of juice and shell to fly across the table and smack me on the cheek. She tore into the creature as if she had a personal vendetta against it, tugging off all ten legs, twisting the claws until they gave with a *poof,* and separating the body from the tail, allowing the gray-green tomalley to slide onto her platter along with a strip of fire-engine-red eggs.

The smell of ocean and carnage filled my nostrils and I felt a wave of nausea. Jack and Ben started devouring their lobsters, ripping them apart and using their teeth to compress the soft shell of the small legs and squeeze the meat toward their mouths, where they could suck it out easily. They tossed the empty legs into a wooden bowl in the center of the table; the shells landed with hollow *thunk*s. Jack's chin glistened with butter and juice.

"So, let's talk wedding," Lily said.

Each time I thought Lily's voice couldn't possibly grow any

weaker, it had. Her words evaporated as they exited her mouth. How did this couple fight, Lily without a voice, Ben unable to hear? I imagined her scribbling her bitterness down on paper, and Ben reading and growling a response.

"I want to know exactly how events are going to unfold," Lily said.

I looked at Jack and started tentatively with the basics. "The wedding will begin at four thirty," I said. Originally, we had planned on five, but Malabar told us it was good luck to marry on the half hour, when the hand of the clock was moving up.

Lily wanted to know the flow of the program: Who would walk her down the aisle? Where would she stand in the receiving line? Where would Ben be? I understood that she was trying to ascertain Ben's and her positions relative to my mother at every moment. She wanted to know how far their table would be from my mother's. Could they face away from her? The goal was to make sure Lily and Ben were kept at a discreet distance from Malabar at all times. There was to be no communication between them whatsoever.

Jack described the string quartet that would usher everyone in, where on my mother's property the ceremony would be held, and the procession to the reception, which would take place next door on the expansive front lawn of the guesthouse. As he drew a map for his mother and placed a star over where the tent would be alongside the house, I wondered if Lily knew how often Ben and Malabar's constitutionals concluded with visits to that cottage. I tried to move the conversation away from the guesthouse by describing the jazz band my father had found for the reception.

"A temporary dance floor will be built under the tent where the dinner is taking place," I said.

At the mention of dancing, something snapped in Lily. Her hands were wrapped around a nutcracker, which was clamped over her lobster's large crusher claw. Lily delivered a powerful squeeze and the claw gave way with a pop, releasing congealed white clumps of lobster blood onto her plate.

"There will be no dance," she said.

"What?" I said, incredulous that Lily was ordering us not to have dancing at our wedding. I had to draw the line somewhere. I wanted Lily to be okay, but this was our wedding, after all.

"You heard me. There will be no dancing between Ben and Malabar," she said, tossing the entire claw, meat and all, into the shell bowl. "The father of the groom and the mother of the bride will not dance at this wedding. Do I make myself clear?"

I understood that Ben's deafness prevented him from hearing this exchange, but surely he could see it. The situation was readable. I looked at him. It was Ben's job, not mine, to assure his wife that he wouldn't dance with my mother. He did not meet my eyes. I looked to Jack for help; nothing there either. I was on my own.

"I am not asking you, Rennie, I'm telling you," Lily went on softly, her rage gathering with a ferocious calm. And then, the eye of the storm: "Tell your mother to stay away from my husband at this wedding."

I felt furious at the situation, at Ben's and Jack's silence, at the thought of our wedding as the stage for some as-yet-unwritten showdown.

"Okay," I said, keeping my gaze on the ruined lobsters.

NINETEEN

I was not looking forward to confronting my mother's heart-break in person; it had been daunting enough from a distance of three thousand miles. That Malabar was suffering was undeniable. In the days, weeks, and months since learning that Ben had decided to stay with Lily, my mother had pivoted from heartbreak to fury, from incredulity to despair.

"I can't believe I've lost them both. First Charles, now Ben," she cried over the phone, repeating herself, as the heartbroken do. "What do I have to live for?"

Her periods of anguish were relieved by bouts of rage. If once upon a time Malabar had quietly hoped that Lily would drift off to sleep and never wake up, now she actively fantasized about her rival's death, an essential part of her happily ever after. My mother felt sure that Lily had been in the room with Ben during his breakup phone call, listening to her husband's side of the conversation, making sure he stuck to an agreed-upon script.

"They weren't his words, Rennie," my mother insisted. "I know Ben too well."

It was Lily's finger, my mother was convinced, that depressed the button that ended their call just a few minutes after it began, truncating their final goodbye midstream. "I was telling him I would always love him," my mother said. "There's no way Ben would have hung up on me. Only a monster could do that to a person. Only Lily."

Insomnia plagued Malabar's nights. She drank more heavily than usual and ate less, allowing her pain to become visible in the hollows of her cheeks and the concavity of her abdomen. Even though I understood that she'd been in the wrong, the way I saw it, my mother had already suffered plenty in her life. It all seemed unfair. I was about to get married; Ben and Lily still had each other, even if in a newly hostile situation. Only Malabar had ended up all alone. I worried that she was suicidal. Or, if she didn't quite have the nerve to kill herself intentionally, it seemed possible that she could do it accidentally—a night of too much booze followed by a handful of sleeping pills.

Ben's love had sustained her for years. Without it, what did Malabar have to look forward to? She was in her late fifties and of a generation and class of women who'd been brought up to feel obsolete without a man. It seemed possible that my resilient and determined mother had reached a point where she'd lost enough of her elasticity as to be unable to bounce back. This mistake, this miscalculation of Ben's commitment, could cost Malabar permanently.

On the drive to Orleans, I warned Jack that the situation would likely be grim when we arrived. I told him that I would probably need to spend time alone with my mother, that she was in trouble. Jack grimaced but didn't object. Since the affair had been exposed, Jack and I had stepped gingerly around the subject of Malabar. I carefully avoided talk of my mother's anguish. In Jack's estimation, his mother was the only one who deserved sympathy, a perspective I understood. I rested my head on the passenger-side window and watched as the backdrop changed the closer we got to Malabar's Cape home, flocks of starlings over birch trees giving way to gulls over pitch pine and scrub oak. An imagined scene between Malabar and me played constantly in my mind: my lonely mother was propped up on a pillowed daybed in a heavily curtained bedroom, a tumbler of bourbon in hand, as I tried to help her imagine a future without Ben.

When Jack took the right turn onto our driveway and the pavement changed to gravel, I took a deep breath to prepare myself. He eased the rental car past the center circle around which the driveway looped and where a gardener was hard at work weeding, trays of plants at his feet. Two pickup trucks were parked on the widest part of the drive, one with its front door open, an oldies rock station blaring. A shirtless worker, balanced on a ladder propped against the side of the house, scraped paint from the trim. Two men in wheat-colored work boots and shorts banged nails into new shingles.

In the center of all this action, sitting on a director's chair on the porch and wearing oversize sunglasses, Malabar waited for us. By the look of everything that was going on, my mother was preparing for our upcoming nuptials as if her life depended on it.

Not a year earlier, a few months after Jack and I became engaged, my mother told me in no uncertain terms that lavish weddings were a foolish waste of money. She didn't need to do much convincing. Neither Jack nor I wanted a big to-do, and we were even less interested in the prospect of managing the details. A deal had been struck: if we agreed to keep things simple, my mother would handle the bulk of the planning. What was a wedding if not a big party? And Malabar knew more about how to throw a party than anyone I knew. Besides, I found tiny decisions like choosing among shades of white for tablecloths disproportionately stressful. Malabar's choices would be exquisite, and I felt relieved not to have to be the one making them.

Malabar waved to us from her elevated perch.

"Un-fucking-believable," Jack said.

"Rennie!" My mother leaped to her feet.

"Mom!" I extricated myself from the car.

Jack got out of the car but stayed next to it, folding his arms over the top of the vehicle's door. "Malabar," he said, nodding as he took in the scene. He made no move to ascend the three steps to greet her properly. This was when I realized that Jack's understandable-but-not-acceptable mantra did not apply to Malabar, whom he now abhorred. "Looks like you've been busy."

I bounded up the stairs to my mother, eager to protect her from Jack's affront. We embraced for a long time.

"I guess a catch-up for you two is in order," Jack said, still leaning against the car.

"What's all this about, Mom? What's going on?"

"Just giving the property a little face-lift for your big day," she answered, stepping back to get a good look at me. "I'm so glad you're here, darling. I've missed you so much." She hugged me again. "Are you ready for the grand tour?"

I turned around to see if Jack would join us, but he was already headed to the guesthouse to figure out sleeping arrangements for his groomsmen and the friends who would be spending the week leading up to our wedding there. My fiancé wanted no part of this reunion.

"You probably noticed the new gravel," my mother said. "Three tons of stone."

"What happened to *low-key*?" I asked.

Malabar laughed and shrugged. "Oh, you know *low-key* isn't really my style. Besides, this seemed like more fun. No expense must be spared for your big day. Plus, it's an excuse to expand the guest list and see some friends. Come on, let me show you."

For the next thirty minutes, we walked around the property, Malabar pointing out all that was under way: what her landscape designer had suggested in terms of shrubs and plants, the sliding glass doors to be replaced, the new trim, a shade bluer than the old blue-gray. Inside, we looked at photographs of deck furniture, options for arched trellises, samples of folding white wooden chairs. When she brought out the menus and photos of floral arrangements for me to consider, I balked.

"Let's wait for Jack on this," I said, overwhelmed.

"Jack's going to have a strong opinion on boutonnieres?"

"Point taken," I conceded. "But let's slow down a bit. I just got here. I'm grateful for all you've done, but . . . well . . . it's a lot. And completely unexpected." At her look of disappointment, I added, "I'm just exhausted from the visit with the Southers."

"No problem. If it makes you feel any better, all this planning has been a wonderful distraction for me." My mother's voice wobbled slightly, and she clenched her jaw to prevent further emotion. "Okay, no decisions today."

"Thanks."

"How about we do something fun," she suggested. "Shall we talk about the dress?"

I was excited and nervous to show Malabar the photographs of my wedding gown. My mother hadn't seemed all that concerned about the La Jolla bridal-boutique debacle. Over the phone, I'd told her how ashamed I felt at having misplaced my trust in the shop owner, how gullible and embarrassed I was at having been played. My mother had seemed uninterested, my wedding-dress trauma frivolous, I imagined, compared to her heartbreak. As we ascended the stairs and headed toward her bedroom, I realized I must have underestimated her interest in the dress. Had I remembered to tell her that the situation had been resolved and I'd found the same gown at a bridal megastore in Los Angeles? I thought I had, but I was no longer sure.

"The pictures of my dress are in the car," I said.

"First things first," Malabar said, opening the door to her bedroom. A grand sweep of her arm guided my eyes to her bed, swollen with pillows, and there it was, centered on her pristine white duvet: the velvet purple case, opened to reveal its mesmerizing contents. I hadn't seen the necklace in years. Malabar motioned for me to sit down on the chaise longue by the window and started to tell me, once again, the dreamy story of how her father had given it to her mother as part of a dramatic second marriage proposal.

I wasn't paying full attention to her words because I couldn't take my eyes off the necklace, how it twinkled and danced in the light. I couldn't believe that she was finally giving it to me, this gemstone-studded collar that I'd been promised for my entire life. *Be very good, and this will be yours!* I had been a good daughter, devoted and loyal, and yet the necklace always felt out of reach.

I knew that children who'd been neglected emotionally, as my mother had been by her parents, often formed attachments to objects instead of people. Malabar had been raised by an alcoholic and domineering single mother, so it came as no surprise that her possessions meant everything to her. This necklace symbolized her mother's love. I understood it; in fact, I felt the same way. My mother was about to give me her most treasured treasure, and the very thought of it made my heart nearly burst. Finally, I would have material proof of her love.

"Close your eyes," my mother said.

I lowered my lids. I heard the rustle of a paper bag and then got a whiff of an unfamiliar earthy scent.

"Okay, open up." Malabar's voice tinkled with excitement.

The purple box had not moved from its spot on the bed. Confused, I refocused my attention on my mother. She was holding up a bolt of fabric, a luxurious sheet of it draped across her arm. It was a raw silk, an iridescent blue-green with hints of purple shimmering beneath. As Malabar moved, the colors changed and the fabric looked alive. Never in my life had I seen more beautiful material.

"It's gorgeous," I whispered, rising from the chair to touch it.

Looking at the fabric was like staring into a mirage, the colors disappearing and reappearing in ripples.

Malabar slipped out of her blouse and threw one end of the material across her shoulder, tucked a fold into her bra, and brought the rest up over her other shoulder, creating a deep scoop neckline that showed off her bronzed décolletage. "I'm picturing a tight bodice and a full skirt." She spun so that the fabric wrapped around her small waist, the colors undulating in the late-afternoon light.

Then it struck me—I'd misunderstood. I had thought we were in her bedroom to talk about my wedding attire, but in fact, we were here to talk about hers. My wedding might be the last chance she would ever have to change Ben's mind.

"The fabric is from India. I'm having a gown made especially for me," she continued. "It's going to be breathtaking." She fanned out a half a dozen photographs from fashion magazines and pointed out details she admired.

"And the pièce de résistance," Malabar said, reaching for the purple box, "will be this." She gently removed the necklace and motioned for me to help her put it on. I clasped it behind her neck.

With her necklace on and tears in her eyes, she told me how she'd gone to New York City the previous month, knowing that Ben would be there for a board meeting and staying at "their" hotel. But he'd rebuffed Malabar when she called and kept his promise to his wife—there was no contact.

Once my mother composed herself, I stood behind her and we admired her reflection in the mirror as we had done so many times before. The image was something to behold. The gems sparkled, and the fabric looked like the ocean bathed in moonlight, shimmering against her skin in an otherworldly way.

I finally understood: My wedding would be Malabar's battleground. She would be radiant, beyond stunning. She would dance with every man and show Ben what he was missing. She would smile, laugh, and flirt—and stand beside my dashing father during their toast. She would be the most glamorous and confident woman in the room. Her secret weapon would be wrapped around her neck, and I wanted her to have it.

"Mark my words, Rennie," my mother said, addressing my reflection in the mirror. "Ben Souther will not be able to take his eyes off me."

TWENTY

July 21, 1990, turned out to be a picture-perfect day for a wedding on Cape Cod. The sun was brilliant; a few clouds scudded across a clear blue sky; a gentle breeze pushed away the day's heat. Nauset Harbor, our backdrop, dazzled with reflected light. Skiffs bobbed on their moorings, fishing boats sped homeward, and canoers silently cruised the marshes.

Upstairs in my childhood bedroom, bedecked in elaborate white underthings and surrounded by my bridesmaids, I observed the spectacle unfolding outside my window as if I were watching a play from the front row of the balcony. My soon-to-be husband, along with my brother, Peter, and the other groomsmen, greeted our smiling guests and ushered them across my mother's fertilized lawn into tidy rows of white chairs that faced a wedding arbor trimmed with delicate tea roses. Beyond the trellis, the bay, dunes, ocean, and sky expanded to form a colorfully striated panorama.

My hair was looped in a chignon, my makeup on; I had only to step into my gown and I'd be wedding-ready. From the window, I craned my neck to see if Ben and Lily had arrived, wondering how my mother was doing preparing for her lover's return. Suddenly, I felt dizzy and put a hand on the bureau to steady myself. Kyra noticed and bolted downstairs to fetch something for me to drink. My other bridesmaids were busily readying themselves—hunched over mirrors, applying lip gloss, and spraying wisps of hair. I sank down on my bed, and the crinoline of my slip crunched underneath me.

Rennie, wake up . . . Ben Souther just kissed me.

I was on the same bed where my mother had roused me out of a sound sleep almost exactly a decade earlier.

Memory is an odd curator. Sitting on my bed on my wedding day, I slipped back to the moment when I'd ceased being Malabar's daughter and became her coconspirator and closest confidante. But time didn't stop there; instead, it kept scrolling backward. All at once, I felt Christopher in the room, a liminal presence I hadn't experienced in years. And then Charles too. And my three deceased grandparents, all young and vibrant. Time crumpled, and specters whirled around me, stirring their ancient dust. The roiling inside me was physical, as if I were adrift at sea with waves churning beneath me. Was this vertigo? Wedding jitters? Or something else?

Days earlier, I'd posed the following question in my journal: Would my marriage to Jack suffer for having been based on a lie? The question was underlined. As was a Rilke quote from a collection of poetry Margot had given me as an engagement present: *"Let everything happen to you / Beauty and terror / Just keep going / No feeling is final."* I wondered if my mother ever stopped to reflect on the remarkable coincidence of her daughter having fallen in love with her lover's son and if she ever questioned the extent of her influence. Perhaps she was unable to. Time had twisted her love into obsession, and my engagement to Jack had become a lifeline for her, keeping her bound to Ben and providing a hope that he might one day pull her back in.

If Malabar had doubts on my behalf, if she worried about my

tender heart, she didn't voice any concerns to me on my wedding day.

——

"You okay, Rennie?" Kyra asked, reentering the room with a glass of orange juice.

"Yes," I said. The ghosts were gone. I took a sip.

"Ready?" She held out my wedding dress.

I nodded and stepped into it, a hollowed-out meringue waiting to be filled. I inhaled and was zipped up, the gown's boning compressing my waist and holding me erect. I stood tall before the mirror, and Kyra clasped a single strand of freshwater pearls around my neck.

"Perfect" came Malabar's voice from behind us. She was standing in the doorway. "Darling, you look beautiful."

I looked in the mirror and saw what she saw.

Kyra went down to assemble with the rest of the wedding party, leaving my mother and me alone. We sat on my bed and she took my hand. I have a photo of this moment, so someone must have been in the room, although I don't remember anyone else's presence. My mother looked glamorous in her shimmering blue-green dress, but it was not indomitable Malabar who was before me. It was my childhood mother, the woman who used to comfort me and tuck me in at night. I had almost forgotten about her existence. I'd been the grownup in our relationship for so long — the one who advised and consoled and did the holding — that I didn't remember what it was like to be held by her. But here was my mom, hugging me, the woman whose soft neck I used to burrow into as a toddler, hiding behind the curtain of her auburn hair. For one brief moment, I was the daughter again.

I'm so scared, I thought, but I didn't say it aloud. Instead, I breathed her in and let myself feel safe. Behind the perfume she'd dotted on her neck to beguile Ben, I smelled vanilla beans and tapioca pudding, childhood scents that lit up a synaptic path to my brain and told me everything would be okay.

—

Downstairs, I took my father's arm. He wore gray slacks and a light jacket with a pale pink rose pinned to the lapel.

It was time.

He squeezed my hand between his arm and warm body, and together, we stepped off the porch and onto the lawn. My gown met the grass with a swish, and one satin heel sank slightly. We faced the driveway, on the opposite side of the house from the ocean. As we'd practiced the day before, we stopped and waited for our cue: the sound of the string quartet. To our right, around the corner and beyond our view, were the backs of our guests. Those who were not craning their necks to watch our entrance were likely staring out at the harbor, which was at its most beautiful this time of day, winking in the afternoon sun. This was the golden hour when the lobster boats chugged back toward Snow Point with flocks of seagulls wheeling behind them, waiting for chum to be chucked overboard. What the gulls didn't catch would descend to the inlet's sandy floor and become dinner for the scavengers below — so much vibrant life invisible.

The Wedding March began.

We had taken only a couple of steps forward when my father stopped me and leaned in close. This was the inevitable moment when a father walks a daughter down the aisle — a moment I'd never thought about because my father was unconventional; he wasn't that kind of dad. When I was a teenager, his biggest concern about my dating was not what might be happening in the back seat but whether I wore a seat belt. "Seventeen-year-old boys are knuckleheads behind the wheel," he'd told me on countless occasions. "Complete fucking idiots." Exactly what bit of paternal wisdom Paul Brodeur would offer at this moment, I couldn't imagine.

It wouldn't be a platitude, because my father didn't have a Hallmark bone in his body. It wouldn't be a blessing, because he didn't believe in God. But I was his only daughter, about to get married, and he'd brought us to a halt for a reason. The stringed instruments continued to play, beckoning us around the corner and past the point of no return, and my father's handsome face broke into a smile. He motioned toward his car, parked on the public landing just beyond my mother's property, a red Toyota Camry station wagon with north of two hundred and fifty thousand miles on the odometer, a point of pride.

"Give me the word, darling girl," he said, "and we can just hop in my old heap and go fishing instead."

I laughed—it was a joke, right?—and suddenly we were both laughing, which had been my dad's intention, no doubt. And we were still laughing a few steps later as we rounded the bend to where two hundred heads turned to greet us. Every face was lit up by the afternoon sun. Every face beamed happiness at us—even Lily's. Margot smiled confidence my way and I held tightly her lace handkerchief, my something borrowed. What reason could there be to feel anything but joy? A laughing bride, young and beautiful, her arm linked with her dashing father's, a handsome bridegroom waiting in the distance. Buoyed by all this love, I felt relief wash over me. The ghosts were nowhere in sight. Everything was going to be okay.

—

After the ceremony, we all meandered across the lawn to the guesthouse, where champagne, a raw bar, and other delicacies awaited. The bridal party posed for some formal, portrait-style pictures and then lined up at the edge of the property under the shade of the lollipop tree where I'd spent so many evenings waiting for Malabar and Ben. Our backs were to the ocean, granting our guests that view as they dutifully filed past, my father the unwitting buffer between my mother and the Southers. I swallowed my first glass of champagne in two large gulps and savored the feel of it washing down into my legs.

———

In the photographs, we were all smiles and champagne flutes. There was not a single candid shot that revealed the mother of the groom staring daggers at the mother of the bride or the mother of the bride looking longingly at the father of the groom. Everyone behaved well, and nothing appeared out of the ordinary. The reception was an extravaganza of ice-cold cherrystone clams, plump briny oysters, curled pink shrimp the size of thumbs.

The wedding album does reveal a metamorphosis, however. At some point between the ceremony and the reception that followed, my mother must have sneaked off to retrieve the necklace. In photographs taken of Malabar during the ceremony, she looked unequivocally proper, as poised as her idol Jackie O., demure in white gloves and a jacket that matched her dress. In photos from the party that followed, Malabar had shape-shifted into an exotic creature empowered by her talisman. Gone were the gloves and modest jacket that had concealed her figure. In these pictures, Malabar was bare-shouldered and graced by all those brilliant rubies, emeralds, and diamonds. Caterpillar to butterfly. She was the most dazzling woman in sight.

———

As the evening wore on and the sky turned a deep purple, the wedding party and guests wended their way from the front lawn to the pristine white tent that had been erected behind the guesthouse, and there dinner was served and toasts were given. The music started, and naturally, Jack and I were the first to take to the floor, dancing to our song, "I Only Have Eyes for You." On the most important day of our lives as a couple, we'd spent virtually no time together. Our wedding was a grand party, but I was—as always—hungry for a moment of connection with him, not easily had on this day.

My father cut in and twirled me away from Jack, who went on to dance with Lily. She was fetching in a primrose-colored dress and matching shoes, and her hair had been set for the occasion. With each song, more guests joined us on the dance floor. At some point, I decided to take a breather and observe the action from the sidelines. From my seat at the wedding table, I watched my father take my mother in his arms and marveled at how the sight of them together still filled me with longing, twenty years after their divorce.

Nearby, Ben bobbed alongside his wife.

And that's when it happened.

My parents met Ben and Lily in the middle of the dance floor and— *blink!* —Ben and my father swapped partners. Ben took my mother's arm. My father took Lily's.

Some part of me had been holding my breath; I'd known that this moment would happen ever since Lily forbade it during our lobster dinner all those months ago.

Had my father cut in on my father-in-law? Had Malabar put my father up to it? Or had it simply happened naturally, like the shifting of a murmuring of starlings?

To my relief, Lily handled the situation with grace. She did not object or make a scene or shoot Ben a reprimanding look. Rather, she focused on my father, engaging him in small talk as they danced, her eyes magnified behind pink-framed glasses.

As for me, I couldn't stop staring at my mother and Ben. Their cheeks were pressed together, words passing in warm whispers from one's mouth to the other's ear, faces aglow in happiness as they enjoyed a fleeting foxtrot against the backdrop of eternity.

PART III

And the day came when the risk to remain tight in a bud was more painful than the risk it took to blossom.

— ANAÏS NIN

TWENTY-ONE

FOR OUR HONEYMOON, Jack and I traveled to Nova Scotia, an oblong spit of land located on the Eastern Seaboard and almost entirely surrounded by water: the Bay of Fundy, the Gulf of St. Lawrence, the Atlantic Ocean. We stayed in Cape Breton in a majestic hotel that sat on a bluff with panoramic views of Cape Smokey and the shores of Ingonish Beach. Jack had researched the trip meticulously, planning daily adventures that included hiking the Cabot Trail, visiting historic sights, and exploring the province's finest restaurants. He made sure we had downtime too, quiet moments to read and lounge in our room, get massages, and enjoy cocktails on the patio where each evening at sunset a plaid-kilted figure marched up the green hillside to blow into his bagpipes, emitting sounds as melancholy and eerie as whale songs.

And it was here, during this idyllic vacation in Canada — where days were not to be hurried through but savored — that a listlessness set in. The most banal of choices left me stymied. Did I want meat or fish for dinner? I couldn't decide. Hair up or down? Either. Would I prefer to walk or bike? Neither. I wanted to sleep. It felt as if in making any inconsequential decision, I might choose wrongly and forever close a door; there would go my other life. More than anything, I felt sapped of energy, the symptom that Jack and I seized upon, the least emotionally fraught issue to discuss on our honeymoon.

"Of course you're exhausted," Jack told me. "Why wouldn't you be? I'm tired too. We just threw a week-long party for all of our friends that culminated in a wedding for two hundred people."

I inhaled his explanations as he exhaled them, a form of mouth-to-mouth resuscitation, an intimate rescue. What Jack said made sense: I was going through a postwedding letdown following so much frenetic expending of energy.

But in my journal, I grappled with how to describe the dimming of my emotions, the way food tasted bland, colors looked dull, and my thoughts were unclear. I wrote that it was like having a small cloud hovering above, impeding the sun's light and warmth. I tried to understand this strange sense of gloom, a steady but seemingly benign presence, more annoying than menacing. Yet whenever I tried to examine it, I found I couldn't quite face it directly. Like the side of my nose, my growing sadness was both constant and peripheral.

On the last night of our honeymoon, I had a nightmare. In it, my brother Christopher had grown into a young man and was waiting for me by the stream behind my father's cottage in Newtown. He beckoned me from the very spot where I knew my parents had sprinkled his ashes. My brother had something urgent to impart to me, but in my excitement to meet him, I embraced him, unaware that doing so was forbidden. All at once, Christopher's body turned liquid and poured back into the creek, now dark and roiling. In the distance, my mother leaned against a tree, hands covering her eyes. She wouldn't look at me. I awoke heavy with guilt, aware only that I had failed her.

As Jack and I packed to go home, I kept returning to the morning after my wedding. My mother had pulled me aside, brimming with excitement about her dance with Ben, eager to fill me in on what he'd whispered to her.

"Mom, please. You have to stop telling me this stuff," I said.

My mother looked crushed. "Why? I thought you'd be happy for me."

"I can't be your confidante anymore, Mom," I said. "I'm married to Ben's son. Don't you get that?" I told her she needed to turn to Brenda or someone else with less at stake personally. "Really, Mom. I'm sorry, but I can't do this anymore."

At my mother's look of shock and abandonment, I softened my tone and explained I was exhausted from guilt and needed to start my life with Jack on fresh footing. It was one thing to have lied to him in the past; it would be more unforgivable going forward. I was no longer a child. "Mom, I'm married to Jack. Lily is my mother-in-law," I said, enunciating each syllable.

"I'm not an idiot, Rennie. I know exactly who you're married to," my mother said, going on the offensive. "It's not as if I'm asking you to murder someone. I was trying to tell you something sweet. Never mind."

"I'm sorry, Mom," I said again, pleading. I didn't want to leave for my honeymoon on bad terms with her. "Please, just promise me that you won't tell me if you two start up again. I don't want to know. I really, truly don't. I can't."

Initially, I felt freed from a burden I'd been carrying since I was fourteen. At long last, my part in the emotional high-wire act of my mother's affair with Ben had ended. I'd been spinning plates for so long that now that all the china finally lay shattered on the floor, I mostly felt relief. Still, I had to be vigilant. I couldn't fall back into my old patterns. Malabar was my Siren and could bewitch me again and again. Deep down, of course, I was dying to know what Ben had whispered to my mother during their forbidden dance on my wedding night. Had he suggested they meet? Had he begged her to wait for him? Already, I missed Malabar and our confidences terribly. I'd been following in her footsteps for so long, I didn't know if I could find my way forward without them.

After our honeymoon, I ferried the cloud back to San Diego, where it expanded inside me over the course of several months, settling in like a moody weather system. I didn't feel sad so much as deprived of my normal range of emotions. Every sensation felt tamped down — victories at work, pleasure from food, distress for friends who were in pain. I couldn't muster outrage when our country initiated the First Gulf War or feel adequate compassion for a colleague whose husband developed a drug problem. In the graph of my feelings, joy and sorrow had inched closer to the median. I had difficulty concentrating at my job and little interest in writing in my journals, something I'd been doing since I was thirteen.

On the surface, life appeared normal. Jack and I had a wide circle of friends and a routine of work and play that included hosting large dinner parties and caravanning across the border to a town south of Tijuana where there was a charming hotel nestled into the side of a cliff overlooking the Pacific. We'd reserve a large table in the hotel's restaurant, drink pitchers of fresh margaritas, and wolf down homemade tortilla chips served alongside bowls of jalapeño-laden salsa and bright guacamole speckled with cilantro. A mariachi band crooned sped-up songs in minor keys, making sad tones sound happy, and our boisterous group sang along to "Bésame Mucho" and "Cuando Calienta El Sol," talking over one another — mostly about nothing, local gossip and sports — until we surrendered to the hypnotic thrum of the waves below, our bellies full of carne asada, our minds blank with tequila. But it was here, surrounded by all these friends, vibrant flavors, and lively music, that I was at my loneliest. I felt as if I were watching myself from above, unable to comprehend the happiness of the people around me.

For Jack's part, getting married had settled something in him, seemingly paving the long stretch of highway ahead upon which we could cruise for the rest of our lives. When Jack looked into the distance, the sight of all those mile markers—our thirties, forties, fifties, and beyond—put his mind at ease. A planner above all else, my new husband had already envisioned and could articulate a clear path to retirement. I was twenty-four; security in my dotage was the last thing on my mind. I wanted off the highway and onto country roads where we could explore, find secret meadows, have sex under the stars. If I saw a pendant at a museum, I'd imagine the love story behind it. If I passed a stooped-over old woman on the street, I'd wonder what her burdens had been. I wept at passages in novels, memorized poems. Jack was rational and practical and coveted stability. He was the most dependable man I'd ever known, but was I looking for dependability?

Margot and I grew closer. She continued to oversee my development as a serious reader, and our conversations about literature became my lifeline. As books emerged as an essential part of my everyday life, beneath the bustle and noise of it all, I was able to listen more deeply. Margot married my father that spring on his sixtieth birthday, becoming my stepmother and a permanent force for good in my life. She was the first person to intuit that I was in real trouble. We didn't discuss my rising desperation directly at first. Instead, we would meet at the café adjacent to her bookstore, where she'd offer literary fiction as antidepressant. She gave me novel after novel: *Love in the Time of Cholera, Their Eyes Were Watching God, The Lover, Vanity Fair*. Each told stories of how characters coped with adversity, bad choices, life's onslaughts.

"Books come into your life for a reason," Margot said as she handed me another stack.

At the time, I didn't quite grasp what she meant, but I craved the escape of plunging into these characters' lives and figuring out their motivations and reactions. The novels wrenched me with their confrontations, pronouncements, and reversals, but they also brought into focus some of my hazy thoughts, providing moments of clarification. Like a woman possessed, I bought packs of three-by-five notecards and started compulsively jotting down my impressions of every book I read. On the front of each card, I detailed my overall response to the book, transcribed lines I loved, and highlighted essential themes, noting when those themes intersected with my own story. On the back, I wrote down words I hadn't known and their definitions.

At Margot's encouragement, I also signed up for a creative-writing workshop taught at UCSD, where, in my juvenile attempts to write fiction, my subconscious revealed its ongoing devotion to Malabar. In an early story called "The Pigeon Slayer," I even managed to create the happy ending I felt my mother deserved. The piece was about an unhappily married hunter who smothers his terminally ill wife with a pillow and thus liberates himself to pursue his great love.

By day, my psyche busied itself with grotesque solutions to my mother's ongoing drama, but by night, it turned its substantial wrath on me. *Fraud. Liar. Fool.* The voices in my head were relentless. Over the next two years, they grew louder and louder until they became unstoppable revenants that intruded daily, most aggressively in the predawn hours, when my defenses were at their weakest. I resorted to drinking goblets of red wine to help me fall asleep. But I couldn't suppress the voices. Each night I would awaken with a start at exactly two o'clock. For an hour, sometimes more, I would lie expectantly, waiting for the endless loop of berating thoughts to end; they didn't stop until dawn inched around the sides of the bedroom shades.

This scene played out night after night with Jack just one foot away from me, sleeping with the peace of the dead. Sometimes I considered waking him up, thinking he might understand and would be able to talk me out of my torment, but he was already confounded and exhausted by my unhappiness. He'd been watching me unravel for months now and was doing his best to support me. He took me for runs on the beach and tirelessly researched articles about exercise as a cure for depression. One of us needed to sleep. I let Jack be.

Everyone close to me knew I was suffering.

"Just tell me what to do," Jack said. "Whatever you need, I'll do it."

"I've been there, darling," my father said. "You're resilient. You'll get through this."

"Let's call my therapist," Margot said. "She'll help."

"Don't listen to the voices at night," Kyra told me over the phone. "They act like they have answers but they don't know what they're talking about."

"Drugs," Malabar said. "Powerful ones. We need to treat this thing with a sledgehammer."

But I also found my depression tedious — tedious to live through, tedious to explain, tedious to be around. I was bored by my own relentless loop and felt sure I was boring everyone around me. I had brought this on myself, after all, having made a series of decisions that landed me where I was: in the wrong city, pursuing the wrong career, and, quite possibly — the hardest thing of all to contemplate — married to the wrong man. What had Jack done to deserve being saddled with this depleted version of me?

I began to loathe living in San Diego with its nonstop sunny days and perfectly fit inhabitants. I missed the messy velocity of New York City and had started to imagine pursuing a career in the literary world. On my bedside table, old political journals had been replaced by current issues of the *Paris Review* and *Granta*. Would Jack possibly consider a life together back east? My husband was happy in San Diego; he loved his job, our home, and his routine. Reluctantly, Jack told me he'd be willing to move, but we both knew that no part of him wanted to leave. Besides, neither of us could say with any optimism that this was where his sacrifice would end.

"I couldn't bear to leave everything I love and then end up without you too," he said.

———

In late November of 1992, just over two years into my marriage to Jack, Lily's heart gave out. She had a heart attack at a restaurant and died on the way to the hospital. Ben delivered the news to Jack matter-of-factly, who told me in a similar manner. I couldn't fathom the concept of being without a mother. It was as unimaginable to me as waking up without the sun. But Jack did not fall apart. He did not cry at the news. Instead, he got through the evening in a high-functioning daze, purchasing airline tickets to Boston through United miles, making an extensive packing list, and calling other family members, delivering the news, and attending to their feelings.

Before the sun set over the Pacific, Malabar telephoned. I hesitated for a moment, wondering if it was my job to tell her about Lily's death. Then the words spilled out.

"I already know, Rennie," she said. "Ben called me first."

I wondered if it was true that Ben had called my mother before he'd contacted either Jack or his sister. Perhaps Malabar simply needed to believe this. She went on to tell me that she'd decided against attending Lily's funeral. Had she actually contemplated going?

In the next room, I watched Jack pace in quiet grief. On the phone, my mother's voice was measured, but beneath the placidity, I could detect the vibrating hum of hope. Malabar would be seeing Ben soon. This love affair, born from a kiss a dozen years earlier, was potentially about to bear fruit. She might finally be getting the life she'd always dreamed of.

I thought of *Vanity Fair*'s protagonist, Becky Sharp, easy to revile for her raw ambition. On the index card I'd made for this novel, I'd transcribed the following quote: *"Which of us is happy in this world? Which of us has his desire?"* Beside it, I'd written *Malabar*. For all of her faults, my mother was a woman who knew exactly what she wanted, something that could never have been said of me. The next quote I wrote was this: *"Are not there little chapters in everybody's life, that seem to be nothing, and yet affect all the rest of the history?"* Beside it, I'd written *The kiss.*

—

Jack and I arrived in Plymouth the next day, a typical New England late-autumn afternoon, cold and damp, the trees naked, the landscape various shades of gray. There were cars in the driveway, and when we pushed open the door, the house smelled of wet coats and stew. A pair of rust-colored mittens stuck out from the pegs that lined the entryway, and Jack hung our parkas over them. Under each peg were the initials of a Souther family member, written in the uneven lettering of a child. Even as a little boy, my husband had craved order.

A steady stream of neighbors and friends, as well as several widows from around town, came and went. They held Ben tightly by the arms or shoulders and shook their heads, uttering words of comfort. There were casseroles and pies on countertops, cards in a basket, vases full of cut flowers that brightened corners. The bounty of condolences demonstrated the community's affection for Lily and the collective assumption that Ben would be lost without his wife of almost fifty years.

When the last of the visitors left in the early evening, Ben turned his attention to us, his family.

"How about a drink?" he said.

There was no argument. This was simply how days ended. It was just the four of us now—Ben, me, Jack, and Jack's sister, Hannah—with some intermittent and welcome interruptions from Ben's siblings and their spouses, who were handling various aspects of the funeral arrangements. Ben made our cocktails, and once everyone had a drink in hand, he raised his glass to toast his late wife. I no longer remember his words, only that they were kind and practical, not in the least romantic or nostalgic.

"Skoal!" we said in unison, Lily's favorite salute. We clinked glasses.

Ben grimaced at his gin and tonic. "This is God-awful," he said and then continued sipping.

Jack and Hannah recounted some family expeditions: backpacking trips to Wyoming and Montana, river rafting and other adventures that highlighted how game their mother had always been with regard to Ben's need to hunt and fish.

When we'd drained our drinks, Jack got up to make a second round and discovered the reason behind Ben's foul-tasting cocktail. Previously overlooked, a strip of masking tape ran along the bottom of the Schweppes tonic bottle, labeling its contents with a skull and crossbones and the words *Plant Food*—written in Lily's block letters.

Jack and I stayed in Plymouth for a few days after Lily's funeral to help Ben organize Lily's things and to go through her treasures and find a keepsake or two. On the morning we intended to return to San Diego, I rose before dawn and slipped into the bathroom. From the second-story window, I noticed a figure on the lawn. It was Ben in a green parka hunched over a dark object, alone. At first, I couldn't make out what he was doing, but I imagined that he was doubled over in grief, crippled by the reality that his wife was gone, ending five decades of life with her. My heart ached for him.

Then I slid on my glasses and pressed my face close to the window. Below me, Ben sat on a stool, his knees on either side of an old barrel, something fluffy and gray flailing in his hands. Birds. Ben had a handful of baby pigeons, their tiny necks clamped tightly between each finger. One at a time, he twisted their heads, slit their throats, and held their bodies over the barrel to allow the blood to drain down the inner edge.

Once all of the birds had suffered their quick and violent deaths, Ben must have sensed that he was being watched. He looked up and found me behind the glass. I raised my hand alongside my face and gave a wave. Ben rose to his feet and lifted his bounty, all those carcasses, high overhead. He smiled at me, his grin enormous. For two years, my father-in-law had been repentant, remorseful for his betrayal. But now, his penance was over. Ben was back—Ben the hunter, the provider, the lover.

I understood then that the squabs would be his offering to my mother. Just as soon as Jack and I turned our backs and were on our way to the airport, Ben would take his leave of the house as well and rush to where my mother awaited him with open arms.

TWENTY-TWO

Back in san diego, I struggled to get through the days. Margot continued to sustain me with novels — *The Handmaid's Tale, Beloved, Mrs. Dalloway* — while also pulling out the heavy artillery and adding poetry to the mix: Derek Walcott, Mary Oliver, Adrienne Rich. I read and read, swimming toward certain ideas as if they were buoys to cling to in the open ocean. My stepmother started to address the topic of Malabar directly, suggesting that I needed to create more emotional distance between us.

"I also had a mother who didn't know how to nurture," Margot said. "You're going to have to learn to do that for yourself."

When I sprang to Malabar's defense as I always did, Margot did not back down. "I understand some of your mother's history," she said. "And I gather Malabar did better by you than her mother did by her, but that's not the point."

I bristled at what my father might have told Margot about my mother's relationship with her mother, feeling protective of their ancient secrets. Could Margot know about their horrific fight, the one that landed my mother in the hospital? Did she know about the necklace and my mother's outsize attachment to it?

"It's you I care about," Margot said. "There's no dress rehearsal here. You only get one life, Rennie, and it's time you get on with yours."

I couldn't imagine how I was going to do that. I was twenty-seven, but I felt so much older, as if the best years of my life had already slipped past me, not fully lived.

"You have to remember that your mother is unaware of what she's done and always will be," Margot continued. "If you're waiting for an apology or gratitude, don't. You have hard work ahead. You need to forgive her and move on. Happiness is a choice that you have to make for yourself."

At Margot's pressing, I sought out the help of her psychiatrist. Beneath her austere accent—German, I think—and frank manner, Dr. B. was gentle and empathetic. She took my distress seriously.

We experimented with talk therapy first. I told Dr. B. about the dead brother with whom I shared a birthday, about my parents' divorce and their subsequent remarriages, about how, when I was fourteen, my mother had woken me to tell me about Ben's kiss and how I'd become seduced and complicit, lying to family and friends. I told her about my abiding guilt for deceiving Charles and Lily and my own checkered history of love affairs and infidelities, including the fact that when I'd met Jack on Harbour Island, I'd had a boyfriend whom I'd essentially stolen from another woman. I also confessed that I'd neglected to tell Jack about our parents' romance even as I made plans to marry him. I left nothing out.

I described the symptoms of my depression, which had now been going on for two years, and the barrage of angry, condemning voices in my head. I even showed her fresh wounds on my arms from where I'd started cutting myself and described the relief I felt from sliding a knife across the underside of my wrist and watching all those red dots blossom into a single line. Voices gone. Pain eased. Peace found.

"Have you ever considered," Dr. B. asked, looking at me over her spectacles, "that because you didn't separate from your mother during adolescence, you are having to do that work now?"

I nodded for her to continue, wondering if she herself was a mother. She looked to be around sixty, Malabar's age.

"I think your depression might have to do with knowing you need to dismantle the unrealistic version of your mother that you hold in your heart. Would you agree that you idolize her?"

Why was everything always my mother's fault? Did I not have agency in this mess I'd made? I didn't idolize my mother, I told Dr. B.; I understood her. I was aware that it was inappropriate for Malabar to have involved me in her affair, but she'd had a hard life—an alcoholic mother, a dead son, a failed first marriage, a second husband incapacitated by strokes before their life together really began, now dead as well. All I'd ever wanted was for my mother to be happy and loved. I felt pretty sure this was what she wanted for me too.

Dr. B. rephrased. "Do you think your mother puts you first?"

My silence answered the question.

Over the course of our weekly sessions, Dr. B. pointed out all of the ways I placed my mother's needs before my own. She would alert me each time I made excuses for Malabar's behavior.

"Do you think it is possible that you might have fallen in love with Jack to please your mother?"

"Absolutely not," I said. I listed Jack's abundant love-worthy qualities. "Malabar had nothing to do with that."

Dr. B. smiled. I wanted to slap her.

When, after a few months of weekly conversations, my depression gave no signs of easing and I was still exhausted and unable to see a brighter time ahead, Dr. B. prescribed an antidepressant. A few weeks into taking the drug, I felt a swell start to form beneath me and found that I could catch the wave and be lifted and propelled forward. These rides were nothing short of miraculous—my appetite back, ideas flowing, the future visible. But the waves soon flattened, leaving me adrift again. Dr. B. tinkered with different combinations of medications—a higher dose of this, a dash of that. With each new cocktail, I marveled at her ability to summon the wind and tide. My mood would lift, and, for a few euphoric days or weeks, I could see my life more clearly. But nothing worked over the long haul. A little lift meant a little fall; a bigger lift, a bigger fall.

—

In Massachusetts, Malabar and Ben joined their lives together at a speed that shocked even our family and closest friends. None of us were surprised they'd found their way back to each other, but given the scandal surrounding the discovery of their affair coupled with Lily's death being so recent, the assumption—the hope—was that propriety would dictate timing. We felt sure they'd wait at least a year before making their relationship public.

They did not.

Ben moved into Malabar's house on Cape Cod within two months of Lily's death. Soon after, they announced their intention to marry.

Jack and Hannah objected for the sake of their mother's dignity.

"What's the rush, exactly?" Jack asked his father.

I begged my mother to wait. "You already won," I said, attempting to flatter her. "You've got the guy. For the sake of Jack's and Hannah's and everyone's feelings, why not hold off, even just a few more months?"

Our collective pleas fell on deaf ears. If anything, our objections seemed to strengthen Malabar's resolve. She refused to budge. Having been deprived of a legitimate relationship for more than a dozen years, she felt she'd waited long enough. And Ben, who had endured Lily's heartbreak for two years, was committed to making Malabar happy. My mother and Ben—sixty-one and seventy-five years old, respectively—decided to marry in early September, nine and a half months after Lily's death.

Ben and Malabar's wedding took place on my mother's property not fifty feet from where Jack and I had married three years earlier. Their guests, numbering around twenty-five, had also attended our wedding. They included Ben's siblings and their spouses, my mother's half brother and his family, and a few close friends. I surmised that most of the guests had known about the affair but also that they assumed they were the only ones in on the secret. The minister, from Plymouth, was a close friend of both families. He'd given the eulogy at Charles's funeral. I wondered if he knew too. I scanned the crowd, fixated on trying to identify allegiances—who was happy for Malabar and who was distraught for Lily.

Ben stood on one side of the reverend, Jack and I—best man and matron of honor—on the other, our backs to the bay. As we awaited the bride, I studied the expressions on the faces of the guests, some smiling, others grim. Then Malabar emerged through the sliding glass doors, radiant in an ivory Chanel suit, clutching a bouquet of pale flowers. She stepped off her deck and started up the aisle toward her husband-to-be. To this day, I've never seen my mother look happier.

Behind her, Jack's sister had tears streaming down her face.

As if sensing the collision of my conflicting emotions, Jack leaned into me and made a joke. "Have you thought about what Thanksgivings and Christmases will be like for the rest of our lives?"

I laughed. The situation was wholly absurd: Our parents were tying the knot as ours was unraveling. We hadn't told anyone; we'd barely admitted it to ourselves. And we still loved each other.

When our parents said, "I do," and kissed, our lives transformed. My mother became Jack's stepmother. My father-in-law became my stepfather. And Jack would forevermore be my stepbrother.

Later, at the reception, I downed two glasses of wine before the hors d'oeuvres even started to circulate. Jack and I presented our parents with our gift—we'd rewritten the lyrics to the song "I'm My Own Grandpa." In the original version, the narrator marries a widow who has an adult daughter. When his father marries that daughter, he becomes his own grandfather. In our version, "I'm My Own In-Law," we lamented the whiff of incest, mistaken though it was, that we knew would dog us for the rest of our lives. The song was a hit, and our family roared its approval, everyone relieved to find something humorous in the occasion.

―

"Does your life feel authentically your own?" Dr. B. asked during a session.

"I'm not even sure I know what that means," I said, increasingly annoyed by our discussions. My marriage was falling apart; I was working as a legislative aide on track to becoming a bureaucrat, which I didn't want to be; and I was living in a town where I felt isolated and misunderstood. I longed for a more meaningful life but couldn't begin to articulate what I meant by this. I felt tyrannized by my desire to be elsewhere and awash in guilt at the thought of leaving Jack.

"It means you're aware of how you are feeling and have chosen the path you're on."

I focused on the cube of amber that sat on her desk, an insect trapped within it. How soon after stepping into the tree sap had that bug realized its mistake? There were no signs of any struggle; all of its legs were perfectly aligned. *Stupid beetle,* I thought.

"Still with me?" Dr. B. asked.

I was, but barely.

I was trying to picture what mattered to me—what was the life I wanted to live? I thought of books, close friends, and conversations that skewed toward life's bigger questions. These were the things I truly cared about, not local political issues, Monday-night football games, or the SoCal beach culture. I blinked. I'd done it. Somehow, I'd penetrated the looking glass and briefly imagined the life I wanted. It wasn't so hard to envision after all.

I had been on antidepressants, to little effect, for around six months when Dr. B. took the bold step of adding lithium to my mood-altering cocktail. The drug was normally used to treat bipolar disorder, she explained, but she'd had success with lithium for patients like me who had not responded adequately to traditional treatments.

When the new drug hit my system, the results were swift and powerful. This was more a tsunami than a wave. Up, up, up I went, as if a whole ocean had been sucked up to form a rogue seiche. From the crest, I could see far beyond my own life. I had a bird's-eye view of not just myself but what felt like all of humanity — but all I could see was futility and despair. After a few weeks on lithium, I became suicidal, fantasizing in painstaking detail the ways in which I might kill myself. Pills were an appealing option, readily available and seemingly not too gruesome, except I had no idea what and how much to take. I found romance in imagining a spectacular plunge from a bridge or a building but couldn't bear the thought of some poor soul having to scrape up my mess. In the end, it was Jack's gun, kept in a drawer in his bedside table, that captured my imagination. I took to holding it while lying in our empty bathtub. I liked to feel the cold weight of it in my palm.

The suicidal ideations were, in the end, what catapulted me into un-expected action. Under Dr. B.'s supervision, I stopped taking all an-tidepressant medication and made a life plan instead: I would move to New York City and attempt to enter the literary world. Jack and I would test-drive a long-distance marriage. It was time for me to chase my own life and find a path away from the wreck.

I can still remember getting out of the cab in New York City and walking toward my new home, toward this strange new life, as if in slow motion. I'd sublet the apartment sight unseen from a friend of a friend. It was on Lexington Avenue in Murray Hill, catty-corner to a Curry in a Hurry restaurant and over a frame shop. Cars honked. Pedestrians marched determinedly. A homeless man sat cross-legged on my stoop next to a cat and a litter of kittens, one of which I would adopt in the coming weeks.

I started up the stairs lugging a single large suitcase. When I made it to the third-floor walkup and stood in front of my door, I took a deep breath. I slid the key into the lock and turned it; it clicked, then released. I pushed the door, and it swung open. From where I stood, I could behold almost all five hundred square feet of my new home. First, I felt the pleasantly exhausted sensation of having pulled into my driveway after being on a long road trip. Then I nearly choked on the feeling of arriving home.

TWENTY-THREE

In the early years of Malabar and Ben's marriage, they went on the lavish trips she'd dreamed of: honeymooning in Italy, chartering a gulet to cruise the Turkish coast, bird watching in South Africa. My mother wrote travel pieces about their adventures that appeared in the *New York Times* and glossy magazines, and Ben glowed with pride at her accomplishments. At long last happily married, Malabar was ready to hang up her apron. She still adored haute cuisine but now far preferred eating out to cooking at home, and her new husband was more than happy to accommodate her desires. Although Ben still hunted at every opportunity, the wild-game cookbook languished. It never found a publisher or a proper home, though it had unquestionably served its intended purpose and then some.

Their first marital project was a renovation of my mother's Cape house that nearly doubled its footprint. On the ground floor, they added a master bedroom suite and an enormous rectangular living room, designed specifically to house a prized oriental rug of Ben's. One of the long walls was composed of sliding glass doors; the opposite one was originally intended to showcase Ben's hunting trophies, his dozens of heads, antlers, tusks, and horns, all expertly mounted. But in the end, Malabar decided she preferred fine art to animal parts, and Ben's trophies were rerouted to a dehumidified room in the basement created for just that purpose.

If Malabar was euphoric about her own life, she was far less pleased with mine. By moving to New York, I was jeopardizing the uniquely modern family she had created—mother and daughter married to father and son. According to her, Ben was upset for Jack and concerned he would see less of his son without me to help lure him back east several times a year. Malabar did not want her husband to be unhappy.

On her first visit to my new home, my mother made a point of allowing me to see my shabby apartment through her eyes. Always discerning when it came to life's fineries, she stepped across the threshold and her gaze drifted to paint-chipped corners, across putty-colored electrical outlets and grimy windows, and onto the solitary light fixture in the kitchen, the base of which held a couple of dead flies.

"I know," I said. "It needs work. A good cleaning. Some TLC."

Malabar looked into the windowless alcove that was my bedroom and at the two stacks of books, all from Margot, that served as makeshift nightstands. She exhaled audibly.

"I plan to build floor-to-ceiling shelves over here," I said, gesturing toward the entry area. "And once my books have a permanent home, I'll get real nightstands."

But even as I spoke, my mother's attention moved again. She looked past the main living area to the kitchen beyond, off of which was a bolted door leading to a rusted fire escape where I planned to grow potted tomatoes in the spring. Under Malabar's scrutiny, the courtyard below transformed into a junkyard, and the single large tree, whose leafy branches I envisioned would paint my windows green in the spring, were revealed as grocery-bag repositories.

"I presume it's quiet, at least?" my mother said, her voice disconcertingly formal.

"Very quiet," I said. "And Kalustyan's is just one block away."
As if the apartment's proximity to my mother's favorite spice shop
made it more desirable.

Malabar had arrived with cheese and crackers and the makings for
power packs: bourbon, vermouth, a shaker, even a lemon to peel for
garnish. The plan was to have a drink at my place and then meet Ben
uptown for dinner. It was a bit early to start the cocktail hour, but
we were at a loss for conversation and I could see my mother needed
something to do with her hands. As she went into the kitchen to begin preparations, I itemized the ugly things she was likely to come
across: peeling contact paper in the utensil drawer, a blue plastic ice
tray, loose faucet handles . . .

The cocktail shaker made a crisp *ka-chick-ka-chick* sound.

"Martini glasses?" Malabar asked with false cheer. "A cheese
board?"

"On my to-buy list," I said, pulling out wine goblets and a dinner
plate instead. Five years earlier, my mother had insisted that Jack
and I register at Tiffany. We balked. The notion of all that formal
barware—the very idea of a decanter—seemed preposterously
old-fashioned.

"Mark my words," Malabar had said to us at the time. "You'll
thank me when you have a complete set of Tiffany crystal instead of
mismatched artsy vases that you'll never use."

Now I was starting over. My kitchen was bare. Guilt had made
me leave everything in San Diego, every piece of china, the silverware, martini glasses, cheese boards; even family paintings and photographs. *I still might go back,* I thought. *Or Jack might move here.*
We were keeping those possibilities alive.

Soon Malabar and I were sitting on my sofa swilling our power
packs and subduing any strong feelings we had. I'd found that getting drunk myself was the best way to handle my mother's drinking.
Tonight, her aloofness was making me anxious and self-conscious,
and the bourbon relaxed me from the inside out.

In short order, Malabar emptied a second large shaker of Manhattans into our glasses and cleared her throat. "Rennie, I have to ask: How exactly do you intend to support yourself?"

In moving to New York, I had left a stable job, a reasonable mortgage, and a partner who had a solid income. I swallowed and hesitated. I had no idea how I would manage. I had some savings, but not a lot. "Well, my hope is to break into publishing," I said.

This elicited a laugh. "Not an entirely obvious way to make a good living," she said.

I had an unpaid internship at the *Paris Review* and was working as a fact checker at a travel magazine, which paid less than half of what I needed to cover my rent.

"I know it might not look good from the outside, Mom, but I'll land on my feet," I said, projecting more confidence than I felt. The truth was, the thought of pursuing a creative life in whatever way I could made me happier than I'd felt in years. "At least I'm not depressed anymore."

"That's wonderful, darling. I'm just curious how you plan to pay your rent." Malabar took a sip of her cocktail. "I need to make something absolutely clear: Ben and I have no intention of supporting our grown-up children."

Suddenly, I understood the purpose of her visit.

"I haven't asked you for money, have I?" But she and I both knew that she was my backup plan. I'd always assumed I could count on my mother if I needed help.

"Not yet," she said, "but you've been making some pretty big decisions without considering the rest of the family, so just be aware that you're on your own." My mother cleared her throat, an indication that there was more to come. "And if you think I intend for my mother's necklace to support your new bohemian lifestyle, think again. That piece is going straight to a museum where it belongs."

I felt like I'd been slapped.

My mother wasn't finished. She went on to tell me that she and Ben had decided to give Peter full use of the family guesthouse.

"It's as simple as this: we no longer want the hassle of renting, and your brother can afford the maintenance and taxes." My brother had an MBA from Kellogg and had already amassed a fortune as a management consultant specializing in telecommunications. Malabar gestured to my apartment, evidence of my inability to contribute.

I wished my head were clearer. I wasn't prepared for any of this. At the very least, I thought my mother would have arranged it so that I could still use the house for a couple of weeks each summer. She knew how much I loved Cape Cod.

I sat quietly for a moment. Then: "Mom," I said, "I think you need to leave."

My mother's expression grew cool. "I'll leave when I'm good and ready," she said, but she rose and went to the kitchen to collect her things. There was the tinkle of melted ice cubes meeting stainless steel as she dumped out her shaker. By the time she turned back to me, anger had transformed her face.

I had seen Malabar's temper on countless occasions—knew the way her eyes narrowed and her chin lifted—but I couldn't recall being the lone object of her wrath. She stood close enough to me that I could feel her breath on my face. I recalled the legendary fight that she'd had with her own mother some twenty-five years earlier. She had confessed to me on many occasions that she'd wanted to kill Vivian in that moment, had described how she'd wrapped her hands around her mother's neck and squeezed. I still don't know how my grandmother, twenty pounds lighter and three inches shorter, found the strength to throw off her daughter and send her stumbling backward into the stone fireplace. Malabar was in a full-leg cast for the duration of the summer, although at the time, she told everyone, including my father, Peter, and me, that she'd dislocated her knee getting out of bed.

Now I had managed to stir some deep rage inside Malabar. Her pained expression seemed to foreshadow physical violence. I was prepared for her to hit me.

Instead, my mother said, "Has it ever occurred to you, Rennie, that I don't want you anywhere near me?"

Given all the compliments and kind words my mother has said to me in her lifetime—and there have been many—it seems unfair that my brain formed such a deep wrinkle around this particular sentence. Why is it that an insult stays with you forever, whereas love and praise passes through you like water through a sieve? To this day, I can relive the moment of this insult more easily than almost any other.

No, it hadn't occurred to me that she wouldn't want me anywhere near her.

Not once.

I thought my mother loved me in the same way that I loved her: with singular and blind devotion. She had been my everything, more important than any partner, including the man I'd married.

But I had overlooked the simple fact that now that Malabar finally had Ben, that hard-won prize, she no longer needed me. My supporting role in her romance was over, and my mother wanted me to exit the goddamn stage. I knew too much about the past, too much about how she'd acquired everything she now had. Malabar had made it to the glorious final act and it was time for the denouement, not for a new plot twist about the daughter's unhappiness. If the essential dramatic question was, Had it been worth it?, Malabar's answer was yes. If there was one truth that I'd learned from all my reading, it was this: Happy endings do not apply to everyone. Someone is always left out of that final, jubilant scene. This time, that someone was me.

—

Following that terrible evening, my mother and I spoke infrequently and saw little of each other. Malabar and Ben's adventures continued, and months turned into seasons, seasons into years. On the occasions that I showed up for Christmas or a birthday, I stayed there only for the meal, not for the week, and rarely even for a night. Technically, I still had a mother, but in every way, I felt mother-less. For the next decade of summers, my father vacated his Truro home for a week or two in August so I could have a house to myself on Cape Cod, the place I still loved more than any other despite the complicated memories it held.

Although the separation was painful, it was long overdue. Dr. B. had been right—in a perfect world, I should have taken flight in adolescence, some fifteen years earlier, and my mother should have supported my doing so, navigating privately whatever sorrows my new independence kindled in her. Instead, at the very age I should have been breaking free, Malabar bound me to her with her secret. And although she'd been the one to initiate our unhealthy dynamic, I had perpetuated it.

Finally, I had the opportunity to change my life. I'd left my home, my career, a man I dearly loved. If I didn't radically rethink how I moved through the world, all that turmoil would be for naught. I needed to notice what was around me as well as within me. I promised myself I'd be vigilant; I'd pay attention to my dreams at night and to where my mind meandered during the day. I found my way back to my daily habit of writing in my journal, less to chronicle events than to compile and order my thoughts. My daily entries went from confessional to revelatory. I wanted to understand what had happened to me and why I'd done what I'd done. Above all, I didn't want to move through life unaware of how my actions af-fected others. I didn't want to become Malabar.

I continued to read obsessively, novels but also nonfiction, works by Joan Didion, Susan Sontag, Henry Miller. Often, my reading felt manic. Desperate to become enriched by books, I sometimes barely remembered what I'd read, yet the unconscious effect of so many sentences felt cumulative, like recurring dreams. A friend who'd noticed the notecards strewn about my apartment gave me an an-tique filing box, perfectly worn with soft corners, to house all these pieces of hope and research. I continued to push myself to learn what words meant and how to deploy them. The more words I had, the more precisely I could communicate my feelings.

But what really enabled me to relinquish the straitjacket of my past was a renewed devotion to friendships. Aristotle famously suggested that through the mirror of friendship, people are able to see themselves in ways that are otherwise inaccessible. This kind of insight happened to me along the way, thanks to Kyra, Margot, and other cherished confidantes. Friend after friend held up a looking glass, and I was able to see myself through their eyes. Perhaps I was not so terrible; maybe I was even compassionate, smart, and a little funny. In the past, when Malabar had been my best friend and singular love, our secret kept me isolated, kept me from being fully known. Now I was opening up, allowing myself to be vulnerable in new ways and accept the company, love, and consolation of friends.

Margot continued to send books and always set aside time for our lengthy soul-stretching phone conversations. I also spent countless hours with Kyra, who was making a life as an illustrator and whose affection and conversation activated my thoughts of purpose and life. There were other friends, too, a bounty of them, all of us bearing wounds from our past that we no longer felt obligated to conceal because we had one another. As I relaxed into these relationships, I felt moored in the rushing stream of life. The loneliness and depression I'd experienced throughout my twenties finally lifted. I learned to become a friend to myself.

TWENTY-FOUR

I TURNED THIRTY in the fall of 1995, and through a series of both random and curated collisions, I was introduced to Francis Ford Coppola—the famed director of *The Godfather* and *Apocalypse Now* —and we discussed the possibility of launching a fiction magazine together. From that conversation and others that followed, *Zoetrope: All-Story* was born. Absolutely nothing on my résumé suggested that I was the person for this job. I did not have a vast Rolodex of literary contacts or a professional history of editorial success. I knew nothing about circulation or distribution, about buying paper or finding printers, about hiring designers or acquiring material from literary agents.

But I had grown up with writers for parents, had a vision for the magazine's success, and felt confident that I could create something fresh. I poured myself into my new job, often working until midnight and beyond, some part of me believing that only literary accomplishment could validate the havoc I'd unleashed in the rest of my life. If I had my father to thank for my work ethic, my mother was a role model for determination: If you wanted anything badly enough, you did whatever it took to make it yours. Period. I finally had a toehold in the literary world; I just needed to stay focused on each subsequent step and not dare look up the mountain.

Jack and I drifted apart, came together, and drifted apart again and again, each time allowing ourselves to venture a bit farther out into the world without the other. Our phone calls and visits became less frequent and at some point along the way, we agreed to see other people, testing the waters of single life while staying married. Our predicament was odd—nothing felt horribly wrong, but nothing felt right either. The essential dilemma for me was whether I could become the person I wanted to be—someone who lived a creative life, openly searching for meaning—within the confines of our marriage. I doubted it. Jack wanted simply to live his life, not examine it endlessly. We were wired differently. In August of 1997, four years into our living at opposite ends of the country, we agreed to divorce, promising to remain close.

Deciding it would be best to break the news to our parents in person, Jack and I visited them together on Cape Cod in early 1998. We hoped to alleviate their fears of a fractured family by showing them that we remained friendly and wanted only the best for each other. Our split would not cleave the family. We could behave civilly at holiday gatherings; in fact, we would be genuinely glad to see each other.

Malabar and Ben had been married just over four years by this time, and although my mother never fully forgave him for staying with Lily when their affair was discovered, their passion went undiminished. They had fallen into an easy domestic routine with traditional roles: Ben made the cocktails, stoked the fires, grilled the meats; Malabar orchestrated the home, their social calendar, and everything else. And although she spent far less time in the kitchen than before, my mother could still, seemingly effortlessly, produce extraordinary meals. On this night, she prepared roasted lamb chops, bulgur tabbouleh, and sautéed greens, a succulent and hearty dinner.

Shortly after we all sat down at the table to eat, Jack cleared his throat and delivered an eloquent monologue on how, despite the affection he and I felt for each other, we'd decided to go our own ways once and for all.

"Have you filed yet?" my mother asked.

Even though my mother and I were still cool toward each other —the fight we'd had in my apartment always fresh in my mind when we were together—I was caught off-guard by the question's practicality. "Not yet," I said. "I mean, we plan to soon, but we wanted to let you know first."

"Well, thank God the decision is finally made." Ben lowered his large hands to the table with a thud. "I don't think I could have stood another year of limbo." He reached for the mint sauce and spooned some over his chop. "Malabar, you've outdone yourself, as usual."

"Isn't the lamb fantastic?" my mother said. "If you can believe it, it's from New Zealand." Then she added sotto voce, "We bought it at Costco."

Jack and I had been living on two different coasts for years, so I shouldn't have been surprised that our parents had anticipated the demise of our marriage. Still, I was expecting a more emotional response, along with some assurance of love and support. Not only were Ben and Malabar unfazed by the news that our marriage was officially over, they were uninterested in discussing the matter further.

What did endlessly fascinate them, however, was the scandal unfolding at the Clinton White House. Malabar dissected the incriminating stain on Monica Lewinsky's blue dress. Ben ranted about Bill's boundless libido. And both castigated Hillary for her unseemly ambition, which somehow, to them, made her culpable in her husband's philandering.

"You know what just galls me?" Ben said with disgust.

Malabar put down her fork and gave her husband her full attention.

"That no one considered Chelsea's well-being. Not for one minute," my stepfather said.

My mother shook her head.

Jack squeezed my knee under the table and we locked eyes. This was the aspect of our parents' affair that had always horrified Jack most: not that they had betrayed their spouses, not the elaborateness of their deceptions, but that they had used me to facilitate their relationship and never acknowledged the pain that had caused me.

A door slammed shut in Jack. I could see it in his eyes. He'd forgiven our parents their affair and tolerated their speedy marriage, but this was too much.

"You know what galls me?" he said, as calmly as if he were asking about the weather. He folded his napkin and placed it alongside his plate. "Hypocrisy." Then he stood, nodded goodbye to me, and left the table and their house for good. In the coming years, Jack would continue to visit his father, but as far as I know, he never stayed in our family home again and avoided Malabar at all costs.

I was not nearly so poised as Jack. Knowing the apology I longed for would never arrive, I felt furious at myself for having thought I owed them an in-person visit. I sputtered some vitriol that left Ben and my mother shaking their heads, confused, no doubt, by my lack of gratitude, and took my leave of them.

———

Once my divorce from Jack was final, I made up for lost time. Having been fixated on my mother's romantic life for so much of my teens and twenties, it was thrilling to focus on my own desires. At long last, I was living the life I wanted and felt at the top of my game. *Zoetrope: All-Story,* birthed in my alcove apartment, now had a sunny office space, a permanent staff of four, and a robust circulation. Not only had the magazine launched the careers of aspiring writers, it received many accolades, including winning the National Magazine Award for best fiction in 2001. I moved into a large and sunny one-bedroom space in London Terrace, an artist-friendly building complex in Chelsea where Kyra also lived.

A far wearier dater than I, Kyra tolerated reports of my romantic and social life with good humor. I wasn't overly concerned with outcomes and found bad dates as entertaining as good ones, as they provided fodder for our late-night conversations. I had a few relationships, some short, others a bit longer — a thwarted academic, a dishonest actor, a creative executive with a bad temper — and all unhealthy. I was drawn to men who, like me, came from dysfunctional families and were wary of commitment.

Then, in 2002, I was set up on a blind date with a man named Nick Keane. By this time, I had been on many blind dates, so I knew not to expect too much. Nick had thoughtfully selected a location convenient for me, a bar directly across the street from where I worked. Should this stranger turn out to be married, alcoholic, self-absorbed, or all of the above, I could easily claim a work obligation and slip back to the office.

But Nick was none of those things. He was forty-one to my thirty-six, intelligent, and attractive, and we fell into an easy banter, exchanging family histories and career paths. Nick had grown up in Kingston, New York, a two-hour drive up the Hudson. He was raised Catholic, adored his parents, and got along well with his five siblings. We had shockingly little in common.

"I guess you might call my childhood boring," he said.

Nick might as well have grown up off the grid in Montana, his stable life was that foreign to me. He told stories of family vacations where eight kids — the Keane children were allowed to bring friends — were shoehorned into a station wagon for twenty-plus-hour drives to Florida, recounting this as if it were a good thing. I couldn't think of a single question to ask about Nick's wholesome childhood. Clearly, the two of us were not meant to be. Nick worked in finance and was wearing a suit and tie. I could already see how this night would unfold: a couple of drinks, some light conversation, a peck on the cheek, and see you never. I could hardly wait to call Kyra; she would appreciate this story.

That said, there was nothing objectionable about Nick either. I was enjoying our conversation and was in no particular rush to leave. Plus, the more I thought about it, the less I bought his story. Who had a totally happy childhood? A challenge formed in my mind. I would give myself an hour to crack my date and unearth his dark secrets. I smiled at Nick, studying him. He had a kind face, black hair, silver-gray sideburns, a ready smile, and dewy brown eyes that twinkled when he laughed.

Sensing my cynicism, he said, "I did manage to have a colossally unhappy marriage, if that helps." But even his horrible marriage had had an upside: two wonderful boys, nine and twelve. Little did Nick know, however, that the existence of these boys put another nail in his coffin — and not for the reasons one might think. As a child, I'd met many of the women my father dated, all fabulous. But invariably I became more attached to them than my father, and when these women disappeared, I was heartbroken. I wasn't going to do that to someone else's children.

When my self-allotted investigative hour was up, I had nothing. I'd dug around and come up empty — no treasure, no corpses. The whole date felt oddly pleasant. Nick was warm and lovely, and, I could tell, already smitten with me.

Too bad I'd never see him again.

"I was married too, Nick," I said as the evening was nearing its end. The waitress had just delivered our check; Nick took it from the table and slid three bills into the folder.

"No kids?" he asked.

"No kids," I answered, smiling. "Actually, it's a funny story. Instead of sharing children, my ex-husband and I share parents." I let this sink in. "Nine years ago, my mother married his father."

I'm not proud to admit that this was a line I trotted out from time to time for effect, to either encourage a conversation or end it. In Nick's case, it was to let him know that I didn't fit into his story.

I needed to alert this nice man that our date was officially over. I would never meet his sons or his perfect family; the gulf between us was simply too vast to contemplate crossing.

It always took a beat for someone to connect these dots, and Nick was no exception. I watched his eyebrows furrow as he considered the information and then lift as he drew the startling conclusion: my ex-husband was my stepbrother.

Historically, my listeners had responded to this with one of two reactions: a pithy quip or a hasty retreat. Nick did neither. Instead, he seemed to absorb the complexity of my one-liner.

"I'll call you," Nick said, kissing my cheek as we parted.

When Nick did call a day or two later, I was at LaGuardia Airport waiting for a flight to California. I was headed to tell Francis Coppola in person that I planned to part ways with the magazine we'd created. We'd had a great seven-year run, but Francis wanted to move the operation to San Francisco and I had made a life for myself in New York City.

Coincidentally, I'd just hung up from a short conversation with another man I was dating, one whose family history was more familiar to me—divorced parents, major mother issues. He and I had gone out only a few times, but already we were playing a familiar game of cat-and-mouse: If I seemed interested, he backed away; if I acted indifferent, he advanced. He was still in love with his ex-girlfriend, which of course I found intoxicating.

"Hi, Adrienne, it's Nick Keane."

Apparently, I hadn't scared him off.

"Hello, Nick Keane," I said, and before I knew it, we'd dived headlong into an earnest conversation. I found myself confiding in Nick about the magnitude of loss I felt in letting go of my literary magazine. We spoke for twenty minutes and then, unexpectedly, my throat clogged with emotion.

"I've got to go," I said, embarrassed.

"Look, I realize we barely know each other, but would you mind calling me when you land in San Francisco, just to let me know you've arrived safely?"

The September 11 terrorist attack had occurred just months earlier.

"I will, I promise," I said. "Thank you for asking," I added. "That's very kind."

For the six-hour plane ride, I sat in a window seat, stared out the oval porthole at the vast dome of sky, and contemplated the two phone calls and the men behind them, one ambivalent, one enthusiastic. There was something about the convergence of these calls, not five minutes apart, followed by this ample chunk of empty time that made me feel as if the universe were demanding my attention.

Margot's words rang in my head: *You only get one life, Rennie.*

This was it, my one and only life. I was thirty-six years old. There were other ways to be. In that moment, I decided to make space for a different kind of future, one that allowed the possibility of Nick Keane.

TWENTY-FIVE

I HADN'T KNOWN that romance without drama was possible. I had only ever understood love to be fickle and fleeting. From my parents, I'd learned that when your vessel started to take on water, you found a lifeboat and abandoned ship. With Nick, I felt the intense psychic fusion of lust and love along with the steadfast assurance of deep attachment.

I married Nick in 2005, just over ten years after I left California. (Jack, who remained a friend through it all, attended the wedding with his new partner.) Nick and I were eager to start a family, and with the prospect of children on the horizon, I longed to return to my family home on Nauset Bay. Orleans was where I'd learned to swim, ride a bike, and catch striped bass. It's where I'd had my first kiss and experienced my first heartbreak. The scent of low tide alone transported me to long summer days spent with my brother catching minnows in tidal pools. I wanted my children to experience it all, to have the same strong connection to the land.

Emboldened by this desire and finally having accumulated a small savings, I made the case to my mother that I should be allowed to share the guesthouse with my brother. In doing this, I failed to consider Peter's feelings, having convinced myself that my brother's substantial wealth would insulate him from injury. He could just rent another house for the balance of the summer, I thought. Hell, he could buy one. I reminded myself that Peter hadn't cared when I'd been the one shut out. But despite my rationalizations, Peter was hurt, and my maneuverings reignited our lifelong competition. Our allegiance had always been to Malabar, not each other; we'd grown up like vines willing to strangle each other for sunshine.

—

I was thirty-nine when I started my family; I gave birth to a daughter and then, three years later, a son. I'd passed the previous decade imagining I'd gotten a handle on my relationship with Malabar, but having children disabused me of that illusion.

Until Nick placed our newborn daughter into my arms, I hadn't realized it was possible for the world to change so suddenly. I sniffed her head, and the intoxicating aroma seemed to fire new neural pathways, unleashing thoughts and emotions for which I had no frame of reference. Had Malabar experienced this when she'd held me for the first time? Or had she been too stunned that I'd arrived on Christopher's birthday? I kept inhaling, attempting to imprint my daughter's fragrant scent into my consciousness. Now that this baby was outside of my body, I didn't know how I could possibly keep her safe. I felt love but also terror. Losing a child was not an abstract idea. It had happened to people I knew. It had happened to my parents.

When the doctor finished sewing up my abdomen, I was rolled out of the operating room and into the elevator, my newborn lying on my chest, Nick walking alongside. The elevator doors slid open with a chime, and Ben and Malabar were waiting on the other side. As my mother approached the gurney, a rush of emotion overtook me, and I was filled with the strange hope that my daughter had the power to heal us.

I was this child's mother now, and at the sight of my own mother, I felt a rush of anxiety that caused me to weep.

"I love you, Rennie," Malabar whispered to me. Then she turned her attention to the baby on top of me, extending the back of her index finger to caress my daughter's cheek tenderly. "Hello, grand-baby."

I felt sure that this new human, so clearly dependent on our collective love, had the power to bring out all that was good in us. It would be only a matter of time before Malabar and I, with the common goal of creating a better future for the next generation, would acknowledge our past. I imagined that my mother would soon come to me and explain herself. I had so much to say to Malabar in this moment, but when I opened my mouth to speak, my weeping turned into gulping sobs.

"Sweetie, are you okay?" my mother asked.

I tried to reassure her, but what I really wanted was for her to re-assure me. I was not okay. I'd waited my whole life to be mothered by Malabar, and now, with this baby in my arms, it was too late for me.

I started breathing in spastic shallow bursts, turning red-faced. I was suffocating. I looked up at Nick, whose expression registered alarm. I couldn't get enough air. Something heavy bore down on my chest and prevented me from taking a full breath.

In a swift maneuver, the nurse sent Malabar and Ben back to a bench in the hallway and turned the gurney toward my room.

"Breathe," the nurse ordered sternly, gripping me by both shoulders and shaking me gently. "Listen to me, Adrienne. Calm down and take a slow, deep breath."

Finally, I inhaled.

She wheeled me into my room.

"What just happened?" I asked once I'd regained my composure.

"You had a panic attack," she replied.

At my blank look, she said, "You were hyperventilating. More air in than out."

"But why?"

The nurse shrugged; she'd seen it all. "Probably it was anesthesia-related. A C-section is major abdominal surgery. Don't worry. You're okay now."

My daughter's eyes were open. I tucked the end of the hospital swaddling cloth back inside the wrap and sniffed her head again. Nick had a hand on my shoulder.

Maybe it was the anesthesia, but when I first saw my mother—as I lay there fresh and raw from having been carved open to bring her granddaughter into the world—the past ran me down. I had a vision like the kind people describe when they're near death. For one brief second, it was as if a curtain had been lifted. I saw a long line of people, faceless in the distance, familiar as they got closer: my great-grandparents, my grandparents, my parents. I was at the front of this row of human dominoes, my infant in my arms, and as my forefathers and -mothers toppled behind me, they pushed the next generation into motion. There was no escape; their collective weight would crush me and my baby.

I had started out as an egg inside Malabar, just as she had begun as an egg inside Vivian, and so on, each of our fates charted from the depths of our mothers. What little I knew about my grandparents and great-grandparents had been constructed around a sturdy fact or two, embellished perhaps by a shy smile in a grainy photograph or an underlined sentence in a book or letter. The specifics of their lives would remain unknown to me, as mine would be to the baby I held. But our collective history would shape my daughter, and there was something noxious in our matrilineal line. Malabar was the only mother I had, but she was not the mother I wanted to be.

Here was my choice: I could continue down the well-trod path upon which I'd been running for so very long and pass along this in-heritance like a baton, as blithely as I did my light hair and fair skin. My daughter could do her best to outrun it. She would grow up to be beautiful and smart and agile, as I used to be, as her grandparents were, as her great-grandparents were before them.

Or I could slow down, catch my breath, and look mindfully for a new path. There had to be another way and I owed it to my daughter to find it.

TWENTY-SIX

ONE MOMENT, I held milk-drunk babies on my lap, caressing the silky tips of their ears as I watched the wind scallop the bay; the next, wobbly toddlers had turned into lanky children who sped past me, running full tilt across the sand, disturbing flocks of gulls and sandpipers feeding at the water's edge. My children spent their summers on Cape Cod just as I'd dreamed they would, making driftwood forts and combing the beach for lucky stones and sea glass. They watched whales surface to spout, dull-eyed sharks slide beneath our boat, schools of bluefish chase frenzied minnows. They became best friends with Peter's daughter, who was a year younger than my daughter and a year older than my son, and the three met each morning at a designated boulder on the bay beach between our houses that they called Cousins Rock. Nick and I marked their growth by carving grooves into a wood panel in our home; up, up, up they soared. Time leaped erratically: slow days, fast months, winged years.

My father-in-law, the beloved patriarch of Nick's large and close-knit family, died in the summer of 2010. Nick and I had been together for eight years, married for five, and our children were five and two. Just before his funeral, his family found an old locked metal box hidden in the basement. The box looked ominous and I felt an irrational fear about what might be inside, afraid of the secrets Nick's father might have kept. In my family, a locked box could only reveal an emotional bombshell—an illicit affair, illegitimate children, a shameful fetish. But the Keanes were excited by the prospect of the contents and went hunting for the key. *Here it comes,* I thought as Nick's nephews pried it open. I braced myself and looked inside. But, no, there was no bomb. No terrible family secret. It was simply a cache of love letters that Nick's mother had written to his father during their courtship.

Then, in February of 2013, Ben suffered a major stroke. The call came from Florida, where he and Malabar had been spending winters for years. I sat vigil with my mother for Ben's final two days and witnessed his soul wrest itself free of his body in three heaving breaths, leaving a corpse in its place. Ben was gone. He was almost ninety-five and had been married to my mother for close to twenty years, their scandalous affair a distant memory.

Two months after Ben died, a year and a half after being diagnosed with ALS, Margot made the careful decision to end her life. Although she was long separated from my father, she remained one of my closest friends and I traveled to San Diego frequently to visit with her that last year. We spoke on the phone regularly and turned to text when she could no longer talk. What would I do without her? Her answer came in her final text message to me, written on the morning of her death: *Where is Nora Ephron when we need her?* I took this to mean "Embrace the mess, live fully, carry on."

And then, most shockingly, Malabar's sharp and agile mind started to slip from her grasp. Although she'd exhibited some minor confusion for a while—a missed hair appointment, an overcooked steak—I didn't see her disorientation for what it was. In hindsight, I can see that it wasn't until her anchor, Ben, was gone that my mother started to drift.

In the spring following Ben's death, I helped move Malabar from Florida back to Cape Cod, stopping first at their apartment in Cambridge, where we spent a few days doing the emotionally exhausting work of sorting through her husband's belongings. We were having a glass of wine in the den one evening when, out of nowhere, my mother mentioned the family necklace.

"I suppose I should just give it to you," she said. "I doubt I'll wear it again."

"Okay," I said cautiously.

Malabar looked at me curiously, then exited the room and returned with the purple case. She opened it and placed it on the coffee table in front of us.

"Here you go," she said unceremoniously.

When I realized that there was not going to be a grand gesture in this exchange—no box within a box within a box, no impassioned expression of love—I felt a moment of deprivation despite the great treasure I'd just been given.

"Tell me how Grandma fell in love with it," I said, attempting to create a meaningful moment for myself. "I adore that story."

"I think it was in Bombay where my mother first laid eyes on it." Malabar paused, concentrating to remember. "She was at home and a peddler came by the house . . ."

"A peddler?" In all the years I'd heard this story, this was the first time the element of a merchant had been introduced.

My mother waved this off. She'd had several small strokes in recent years and spoke hesitatingly, often using words that were close to but not precisely what she meant. She continued the story until it reached its familiar end: my grandfather on bended knee proposing to Vivian for the second time. My mother, their only child, witness to their extraordinary and flawed love.

In the silence that followed, I picked up the purple case, turned it once in my hands, and gently closed the lid. "Thank you, Mom. This means so much to me."

"What are you doing?" she said, laying a proprietary hand on the velvet box. "It's yours, but that doesn't mean you can just leave with it."

"Why not?" I was taken aback.

"Well, it won't be safe in New York." Now both her hands were on the box, exerting a mild resistance, suspending it between us.

"Of course it will." I paused. "Mom, are you giving me the necklace or not?"

"I am. But I still don't think you should take it."

"If it's mine," I said, freeing the case from Malabar's grip with a quick tug, "I'm taking it to New York to get it appraised."

"Oh, Rennie," my mother said, as if I'd just confirmed her greatest suspicion of me. "You still don't get it. The necklace is priceless. It's un-appraisable."

Back in New York, I did my due diligence and tracked down the contact information of the foremost expert on Indian antiquities at Christie's auction house. But instead of pursuing the appraisal, I stashed the necklace in the back of my own closet and tried to forget it was there. I suppose that, like Malabar, I didn't want to know the truth. If my mother was right and the necklace was worth millions, I knew someday I would betray her by selling it; Nick and I were not financially well-off enough to keep possession of something of such value. And if she was wrong and the necklace was worthless, I didn't think I could bear to know that the fairy tale I'd grown up with had been a figment of Malabar's imagination run wild.

—

The following summer, just over a year into my mother's widowhood, what she thought was a spider bite on the back of her arm turned out to be something more sinister. Her local dermatologist sent her directly to a melanoma expert at Brigham and Women's Hospital in Boston, where I accompanied her on an arduous day of appointments. She saw a dermatologist, an oncologist, and a surgeon and had a PET scan. When the oncologist spoke to us at the end of the day, he told us my mother had an aggressive spindle-cell melanoma and prepared us for the worst.

In a daze, I drove Malabar back to Cape Cod. We inched along in Friday-afternoon rush-hour traffic. My mother was silent, staring out the passenger window into the middle distance. I couldn't tell if she was absorbing the news or denying it.

On the Cape, Nick and our children awaited my return. We had plans to celebrate our daughter's birthday that weekend, a date that always marked the bittersweet end of summer. The light had already started to change over the marsh, and in the coming weeks, we'd close up our house, haul in our skiff and mushroom anchor, yank spent tomato plants, scatter mouse traps in the basement. I wondered how I'd leave Malabar to face cancer alone that winter.

"Do you want to talk?" I asked.

Lost in her thoughts, Malabar shook her head.

When we passed Plymouth, the halfway mark, I tried again. "What are you thinking about, Mom?"

She sighed. "Christopher. I was just wondering if my mother was looking after him."

"What do you mean?" I asked.

"I'm not really sure," she said. "I just hope my mother's taking care of him. He was so little when he died. I don't know. My mother . . ." Her voice trailed off, a frequent occurrence these days.

"Go on," I said encouragingly, suddenly eager to have this conversation, desperate to feel connected to her.

"How to put it? I know my mother loved me," Malabar said, carefully choosing each word, "but not so much as she loved herself."

My breath caught in my chest.

We were about to embark on the conversation I'd been waiting my whole life to have, the one I'd thought we might have on the day my daughter was born. I was the exact same age this summer as Malabar had been the summer Ben Souther first kissed her. How quickly she'd decided to change her life course in that moment, tacking to catch a new wind, with me tangled in the riggings. How I wished I could speak to my mother from the same age, forty-eight-year-old to forty-eight-year-old, to understand what she was thinking the night she woke me up. I thought of my own daughter and tried to imagine circumstances where I might do the same: *Wake up, please. Wake up.* Not a single one came to mind.

"What you just said about your mother, Mom," I said, without a trace of accusation in my voice, "is exactly how I feel about you. I know you love me, but maybe not so much as you love yourself."

I inhaled and pressed my lips together. If Malabar was going to get angry or defensive, it would happen now. She did not. Instead, she seemed to take it in. She was going to give me this at last, our reckoning.

I felt emboldened to continue, even as tears blurred my vision. "I've always felt you came first, your possessions and passions," I said, "and I was secondary."

I willed myself to stop talking. I waited for her to explain to me how I'd gotten it wrong or, at the very least, to tell me how sorry she was that she'd repeated her mother's mistakes. Surely her diagnosis of cancer would grant her the clarity to see that family was more important than property.

Miles of highway vanished under our wheels before Malabar spoke again. Then she said this: "Rennie, I know you're going to be mad at me" — pause — "but I want my necklace back."

I must have misheard. I had to have.

"I want my necklace back," my mother repeated.

I stared straight ahead, reeling from the landslide of her simple sentence. My hurt felt bottomless. I pictured every conceivable way I could wound her: I'd never speak to her again. I'd keep my children from her. I'd sell the necklace. I'd throw it into the harbor. I'd strangle her with it.

When Malabar finally understood my silence as rage and realized the gravity of her misstep, I took pleasure in her rising panic. In the months since Ben's death, I had been there for her as no one else had. I called daily and was a constant source of compassion. No longer.

"Honey, just keep it. Keep the necklace," she said, backpedaling. "Let's just be friends again."

Not in a million years, I thought.

Malabar begged me to forgive her, and in her growing hysteria, she explained that her own mother, dead for over thirty years, was furious at her for giving me the necklace.

Malabar's mother, I began to see, was just as indomitable a presence for her as she was for me. I wondered what my mother had endured as a child. If Vivian was capable of breaking her adult daughter's leg in a drunken rage, what fury might she have unleashed on Malabar as a little girl?

By the time I pulled into her driveway, an hour later, my anger had subsided into sadness. My mother was a widow for a second time. She'd just been given what we all thought was a terminal diagnosis. She was increasingly confused. The summer was coming to an end, and my family and I would be going back to New York City soon, leaving her to fend for herself.

I was exhausted, ready to collapse. *Enough* was the feeling that radiated from within me. *Enough. Enough. Enough.*

I helped my mother out of the car and she took my arm to steady herself as she climbed the three steps to her front door, the same threshold Ben had crossed with his bloodstained bag of pigeons all those years ago, announcing his presence by calling out *How do!*

"You know, I'm sorry for all of this, Rennie," she said. "I love you to pieces. More than anything else in the world."

I nodded. I knew Malabar loved me as much as she could love anyone.

I said good night to my mother and found my way in the dark to the path that cut through the thicket of brush between our houses, to Nick and the family we'd created together. Upon my return, my daughter wrapped her arms around me, happy to have me home, excited for her upcoming ninth birthday. Nick joined our embrace, enveloping the two of us from the outside, and then our son wormed his way into the middle, his favorite spot.

We swayed in this position for a moment, a tight circle on the deck, the dark sky pinpricked by starlight. All I ever wanted was right here. As I embraced my husband and children, I realized that I'd broken the chain. I was still Malabar's daughter, of course. And while I knew I would never abandon her — that when she called, I would always answer, until the end — I also knew that I'd escaped her hold. We were not, as I had grown up believing, two halves of the same whole. She was her own person, as was I. And I knew that every time I failed to become more like my mother, I became more like me.

EPILOGUE

EVERY SUMMER BACK on Cape Cod, I take long walks on Nauset's outer beach in search of sea glass for my collection. I avoid anything sharp or shiny, having trained my eyes to scan for muted nuggets in shades of blue, brown, and green. Imagine, a jettisoned and broken bottle, tumbled by waves, weathered by sand, etched by salt, returning to shore, where beauty is found in its scars. My children and I like to speculate about the origins of each piece, envisioning the moment when it was hurled into the sea.

The question of origins—of where one begins—determines so much. I started this account with my mother's kiss. How different would this story be if I'd started it on the day my brother Christopher died in my mother's arms? Then Malabar would have elicited sympathy from readers, admiration for the courage it took to carry on. My mother is nothing if not a survivor. The life-threatening melanoma has not returned, but having been spared one terminal diagnosis, she is now sinking day by day into the abyss of dementia.

I am fifty-three. For all the years I spent burying my mother's secrets, I've now spent at least as many excavating them. There is so much to look at, so much to hold up to the light—infidelities, addiction, a lost child, and, above all, the deprivation that comes from not being known. Malabar is no longer able to help me find answers, but she smiles when I read passages aloud from these pages, relishing those days when she was a powerful woman who went after all that she wanted. I skip over the parts where she failed me, but I know they are there.

It's said that if we do not learn from the past, we are condemned to repeat it. And that fear — coupled with the desire to be a different kind of mother — has compelled me to wade through the raw material of my mother's life as well as my own, salvaging whatever plunder and treasure I can before the tide buries the wreck again.

My daughter is almost fourteen, the age I was when my mother woke me to tell me about Ben's kiss. And although she and I bear a strong resemblance to each other — bone structure, build, coloring — my daughter is fully herself, with a ready laugh and a bright singing voice that neither her grandmother nor I possess. She and her grandmother have always had a special bond, one that is pure, because Malabar is no longer capable of wielding love to her advantage.

Sometimes I want to ask my daughter, *Are you okay? Am I getting this right?*

The answer came not long ago when she walked into my study, perplexed by an English assignment. She was tasked with writing an essay about a personal challenge she'd had to overcome herself, a time when the adults in her life were unavailable and she'd had to handle matters on her own.

"I don't get this," she said, apparently mystified at the thought of parents who were absent or unsupportive.

I thought of all those moments my parents were absent, and I blinked back tears.

"Mom, what would you write if you were me?"

ACKNOWLEDGMENTS

For believing, thanks to Brettne Bloom and Lauren Wein, literary agent and editor extraordinaire, respectively. This book would not exist were it not for their advocacy, insight, and friendship.

For taking the time to read and provide commentary, thanks to Julie Costanzo, Kathryn Shevlow, and Leslie Wells. For reading every draft multiple times, heartfelt thanks to Carole DeSanti, Sarah Rosell, and Zoe Thirku.

For love and encouragement, thanks to my modern family: my husband and heart, Tim Ryan, and our children, Madeleine and Liam Brodeur, who tiptoed around our apartment so as not to disturb me as I wrote; Chris Brewster, who verified facts, provided photographs and letters, and was unwavering in his support; his partner, Valerie Due, for embracing the madness; Milane Christiansen and Maggie Simmons, whose love and wisdom guided me through my darkest hours; Bill Brewster and Harry Hornblower, both of whom I adored; Stephen Brodeur, who experienced the other side of this (his story to tell); Andrea and Olivia Brodeur, sunshine in human form; Hank, Hatzy, and Gusty Hornblower, Eleanor Sarren, and Holly Brewster, kind people with whom I shared this complicated clan; Marie and Bill Ryan, exemplary role models; Tim and Nick Ryan, extraordinary young men.

For friendship, thanks to Kenna Kay, who has seen me through thirty years of highs and lows; Jodi Delnickas and Cobina Gillitt, without whom I wouldn't have survived my teens; Eilene Zimmerman, who's been writing alongside me since we were in our twenties; Rebecca Barber, Kristen Bieler, and Alisyn Camerota, the momfriends I didn't know I could hope for; and the bevy of literary comrades who've encouraged and inspired me along the way, including Pinckney Benedict, Lea Carpenter, Isa Catto, Julie Comins, Scott Lasser, Emily Miller, Sara Powers, and Peter Rock.

For their hard work in bringing this book into the world, thanks to the team at Houghton Mifflin Harcourt: Ellen Archer, Helen Atsma, Larry Cooper, Debbie Engel, Candace Finn, Pilar Garcia-Brown, Lori Glazer, Maire Gorman, Hannah Harlow, Bruce Nichols, Tracy Roe, Taryn Roeder, and Christopher Moisan. Thanks also to the Book Group: Julie Barer, Faye Bender, Elisabeth Weed, Dana Murphy, Hallie Schaeffer, Nicole Cunningham; my foreign agent, Jenny Meyer; my legal team, Jesseca Salky and Heather Bushong; and the film team, Peter Chernin, Josie Freedman, Kelly Fremon Craig, Dani Bernfield, and Chris Lupo; and Michael Taeckens of Broadside Media.

For their support, thanks to my colleagues at Aspen Words: Marie Chan, Elizabeth Nix, Ellie Scott, and Caroline Tory; at the Aspen Institute (too many to list): Elliot Gerson, Janice Joseph, Linda Lehrer, Jamie Miller, Eric Motley, Dan Porterfield, and Jim Spiegelman; and on the Aspen Words advisory board (past and present): Tom Bernard, Suzanne Bober, Sandie Bishop, Kitty Boone, Chris Bryan, Tara Carson, Gretchen Cole, Paul Freeman, John Fullerton, Sue Hopkinson, Jill Kaufman, Marcella Larsen, Erin Lentz, Todd Mitchell, Beth Mondry, Sue O'Bryan, Cathy O'Connell, Blanca O'Leary, Arnold Porath, Barbara Reese, Lisanne Rogers, Sarah Chase Shaw, Mark Tompkins, and Linda and Denny Vaughn.

ACKNOWLEDGMENTS

For the time and space to get my footing on this dream, thanks to Hedgebrook.

For daily inspiration, thanks to Brain Pickings.

For attention to body and soul, thanks to Johanne Picard and Katie Dove.

For all else and above all, thanks to my parents, Paul Brodeur, who showed me that a life in literature was possible, and Malabar Brewster, my first and most abiding love.